VOICES IN THE WILDERNESS

Emerging Roles of Israeli Clergywomen

Voices in the Wilderness

Emerging Roles of Israeli Clergywomen

Edited
Jonathan L. Friedmann and Meeka Simerly

Gaon Books
www.gaonbooks.com

For permissions, group pricing, and other information contact
Gaon Books, P.O. Box 23924
Santa Fe, NM 87502
or write gaonbooks@gmail.com.

Manufactured in the United States of America.
The paper used in this publication is acid free and meets all ANSI (American National Standards for Information Sciences) standards for archival quality paper. All wood product components used in this book are Sustainable Forest Initiative (SFI) certified.

Library of Congress Cataloging-in-Publication Data

Voices in the wilderness : emerging roles of Israeli clergywomen / edited by Jonathan L. Friedmann and Meeka Simerly.
    pages cm
 Includes bibliographical references and index.
 ISBN 978-1-935604-67-9 (pbk. : alk. paper) -- ISBN 978-1-935604-68-6 (ebook)
 1. Judaism--Functionaries. 2. Women rabbis--Israel. 3. Rabbis--Israel. 4. Women cantors (Judaism)--Israel. 5. Cantors (Judaism)--Israel. I. Friedmann, Jonathan L., 1980- editor.
 BM652.V65 2014
 296.6'1082095694--dc23
                    2014034679

Table of Contents

PREFACE

At Osah Mah *Be'America*? You Do *What* in America?

Meeka Simerly

THE IDEA OF DOING A BOOK ON THE ROLE OF ISRAELI and Israeli-born clergywomen began during a visit to Israel in the summer of 2010. I was invited to a class reunion and reconnected with childhood friends I had not seen for twenty-five years. After being asked repeatedly "*At osah* mah *be'America*?" (You do *what* in America?), it became clear that many people in Israel lack an understanding of the role of women clergy in that country and in the Diaspora. Being a woman Reform cantor is difficult for Israelis to comprehend: in my everyday life I dress and look like any other "secular," but in the synagogue I wear a *talit* and *kippah*. I sing, speak, read and think in my native language, modern Hebrew, but I also know prayers from *Kaddish* to *Shmoneh Esreh* and *Kol Nidrei* word by word.

The eclecticism of my background is apparent in the library of songbooks and sheet music I have been collecting since childhood. It consists of a variety of secular Israeli and non-Jewish songwriters like Yehudit Ravitz, Naomi Shemer, John Denver, The Beatles, Shlomo Grunich, and folk-rock collections from the 60s to the 90s, as well as a wide assortment of old and contemporary Jewish religious music from composers like Debbie Friedman, Abraham Idelsohn, Lisa Levine, Jeff Klepper, Craig Taubman, Aminadav Aloni, Rachelle Nelson, Max Janowsky, and others.

With the polarities of growing up "ultra secular" in a Zionist Israeli environment to now serving as a Reform cantor in the United States, I realize how different and confusing my path is for many people, including my own family members in Israel. This uniqueness has made me feel somewhat isolated but has also made me curious about other women's experiences both in Israel and the United States. We have the growing contrast in Israel between religiously dogmatic women throwing stones at other women in the Kotel Ha'ma'aravi (The Western Wall) to the visible trend of provocative young women dressed in mini-skirts and espousing the "YouTube-star-for-a-day" ethos.

I wanted to find out how other Israeli clergywomen, who represent a group of increasingly influential women, have evolved into their unique roles in religious practice. How do they deal with professional and personal struggles? What are the rewards that come with their work? I wanted to reach out and connect with other women like myself and find answers. So, on the flight home to America following that trip in 2010, I decided to explore this subject in more detail.

I felt I could not embark on this project alone, so I turned to my colleague and collaborator Cantor Jonathan Friedmann,[1] whom I had met at the Academy for Jewish Religion, California. Though we were both cantorial students in a relatively small program, our paths hardly crossed outside of the few classes we took together. In 2008, while working on my thesis and recital, I was looking for someone to write musical arrangements for my thesis subject, which wove together Naomi Shemer songs expressive of a variety of traditional, liturgical, Zionist, and modern Jewish influences that told Shemer's life story. (The result was a religious service with readings, prayers, and music.) From our mutual voice teacher and mentor Cantor Perryne Anker, I learned about one of Jonathan's many hidden talents: in addition to being a cantor, cellist, highly prolific writer and editor, Dr. Friedmann is also an arranger! Not knowing what kind of a response to expect, I turned to him asking for help. After I explained what I had in mind, he agreed and a new partnership was born.

Jonathan wrote most of the vocal and instrumental arrangements for my program and also played cello and sang during my presentation. Before our graduation, Jonathan asked how I felt about submitting my thesis to him to be condensed into a book chapter. Since then we have been collaborating on other projects, and I knew that for the new idea that was brewing within me, I wanted to work with no one else. So the long process of gathering information and approaching potential candidates began in January of 2012.

Since then I have learned so much from other Israeli clergywomen, some I have met in person and some I hope to meet one day. Of course, I was concerned at first whether the women clergy that we approached would respond. I wondered whether it would be worth publishing. I asked if these very busy women would say "yes" to strangers they had never met before. But after reading the essays by the first women who responded, I knew that Jonathan and I were on the right track.

The women, who have written here, have been a great inspiration for me, helping me formulate my own thoughts and share the story of my own journey. Their enthusiasm and willingness to explore and expose their inner struggles, painful challenges and humorous encounters gave me the encouragement and "push" I needed.

My desire to advance awareness of the significant role of Israeli women in the until-recently exclusively male realm of Jewish religious leadership was strengthened when I read an article in *Yediot Achronot* (an Israeli newspaper) about women Israeli Air Force pilots—who have earned almost the same status as men pilots (almost, but not quite). If Israeli women pilots, why not Israeli women cantors and rabbis?

I would like to thank all of the wonderful people who are such an important part of my life. You have contributed to shaping the woman I have become, the woman I am becoming, and the woman I strive to grow into being. Foremost is my loving and supportive husband, Dave Simerly. You are the light of my life. I also owe gratitude to my family, colleagues and friends in Israel. And I would like to thank my friends and colleagues in the United States, and my current community of Temple Emanu-El in San Jose.

I am dedicating this book to all Jewish clergywomen, wherever you are: For your courage, dedication, love of Judaism, and for not abandoning hope that even in a male-dominated world, our voices have been and will be heard. For future generations of women who will strive to become whatever they wish: allow a Calling to manifest itself. *Yi'shar ko'cha'chen gam ne'shot ha'kotel*! Your courage is inspiring.

NOTES

1. Meeka Simerly, "Naomi Shemer's Artistic Expression: Poetry, Prayer, or Both?" in *Emotions in Jewish Music: Personal and Scholarly Reflections*, ed. Jonathan L. Friedmann (Lanham, MD: University Press of America, 2012), 5-29.

INTRODUCTION
Your Voice is Sweet
Jonathan L. Friedmann

O N SEPTEMBER 5, 2011, AN IDF ENTERTAINMENT TROUPE performed at a military event at Ba"had Echad,[1] an officers' training base in the Negev region of southern Israel. When a female soldier began to sing a solo, nine observant cadets left in protest, claiming it was forbidden for them to hear a woman sing. Their regiment commander chased after them and ordered them to return. Four cadets refused and were dismissed from the officers' training course. Following this highly publicized incident, Yonah Metzger, the Ashkenazi Chief Rabbi of Israel at the time, issued a *responsum* justifying the soldiers' protest and demanding that the IDF only allow men to sing at military events attended by Orthodox Jews. Other prominent rabbis were quoted in the media as supporting or opposing the soldiers' actions. Their divergent opinions mirrored the mixed reactions of observant cadets present at the ceremony, several of whom did not walk out.[2]

Contrast this controversy with the Jewish reality in America, where the Orthodox minority (roughly ten percent) has little significant sway on general Jewish matters, save for the standards of *kashrut* to which food manufacturers abide. Egalitarianism in Jewish religious life is the overwhelming norm. Few object to women serving as synagogue leaders, girls having bat mitzvah ceremonies, women training for clergy positions, or anything else. In the decades since rabbinic and cantorial ordinations/ investitures were opened to women in non-Orthodox movements, the number of female seminary graduates has kept pace with or exceeded that of males. For instance, of the thirty-one rabbis ordained in 2013 by the Reform movement's Hebrew Union College–Jewish Institute of Religion, fifteen were men and sixteen were women. All ten of its cantorial ordinees were women. That same year the trans-denominational Academy for Jewish Religion,

California ordained one female cantor, five female rabbis and just two male rabbis. (The Academy is also the first Jewish seminary to have as its president an Orthodox woman, Tamar Frankiel. Only in America.)

The Reform movement ordained its first female rabbi in 1972, and the Conservative movement followed in 1985.[3] Reform cantorial investiture (now ordination[4]) first opened to women in 1975, and the Conservative movement began investing women cantors in 1987.[5] The gradual embrace of clergywomen in liberal Jewish communities is a complex and multi-layered socio-historical phenomenon, the intricacies of which cannot be fully addressed here. Suffice it to say that, while these decisions were hotly debated, they came as part of a larger awareness of women's personhood and struggle for equal treatment (a vision that has had great realizations, but still faces major challenges). Blu Greenberg, co-founder of the Jewish Orthodox Feminist Alliance and proponent of expanded opportunities for women within the framework of Jewish law, included the following observation in an essay written in 1987, the year women were welcomed into the Conservative cantorate. Her encapsulation of the driving ethos warrants lengthy quotation:

> *[B]eyond the orthodox community, in the broader society, there is a new way of looking at women today: as part of her dignity and personhood a woman should be able—and encouraged—to fill all roles that are not gender specific; that no role should be closed to her merely because of her sex. Translated, this means that a woman who hears the religious calling could and should be able to carry the congregation in prayer, could and should assume a leadership role in communal liturgy as she has so assumed in the fields of education, business, politics or volunteer organizations. More than that, one who desires to serve God and community should be welcomed and not pushed away. What, after all, does it require to be a* sheliach tzibbur *[messenger of a congregation]? Voice or gender is not the critical issue. Understanding, inspiration, piety,* kavanah *[devotional intention] are.*[6]

What led to restrictions on women's song in the first place? This, too, is a topic much larger than can be justly explored here. As referenced in the wake of the cadet ceremony, opinions about listening to women's voices are not uniform within the wide umbrella of Orthodox Judaism. Without getting bogged down in *halakhic* (legal) minutia, it should be noted that some forbid hearing a woman sing under any circumstances, while others avoid hearing a woman while reciting the *Sh'ma* (the Jewish proclamation of faith).[7] Either way, the traditionalist consensus is that the synagogue is no place for a woman's voice.

The textual basis for this rule comes from an exhortative statement of Rabbi Sh'muel, a third century Babylonian sage (ca. 220 C.E.). Sh'muel searched for a biblical hook upon which to hang his view that a woman's voice is seductive—a view not uncommon in his culture and, we might conclude, among his rabbinic colleagues. He found it in a verse from Song of Songs, in which a young man pleads to his beloved: "Let me hear your voice for your voice is sweet" (2:14). Using an interpretive method common in Talmudic discourse, Sh'muel rearranged the letters in the word *arev* ("sweet") to read *erva* ("indecent"—i.e., sexually stimulating), thus transforming a romantic and glorifying verse into a dire warning: "A woman's voice is indecent" (Berakhot 24a).

Interestingly, this obscure and seemingly idiosyncratic remark was not presented as a law and was not further elucidated in the Talmud. That did not prevent later authorities from grabbing hold of it, presumably because it resonated with misogynistic sentiments pervasive in their own cultural milieus. Again, some took the extreme position that a man should never listen to a woman sing, while others suggested that a woman's voice should not be heard during prayer. From these varied discussions evolved the principle of *kol isha* ("the voice of a woman"), which at minimum bans women from religious singing.

Kol isha is part of a larger assortment of restrictive customs, the sum total of which resulted in the barring of women from the Jewish clergy. These customs include the release of women from time-bound ritual obligations (ostensibly to allow them to care for their children), the separation of women and men in public prayer (to keep men from lustful thoughts during prayer), and related instructions concerning women's modesty in appearance (reinforcing the desire that women keep a low public profile). Chief among these is the exemption from time-bound positive commandments, including public worship, which is interpreted to render a person ineligible to pray on another's behalf—the central ritual function of rabbis and cantors.

In the United States, where Jewish expression is voluntary and denominationally diverse, individuals may choose to align themselves with Orthodoxy, identify with a more progressive system or abstain from formal affiliation. With the free exercise of religion, each of these permutations falls outside the parameters of governmental control, making Jewish identity a very personal matter. If one affirms the principle of *kol isha* and the broader array of Orthodox legalism, that option is available. If one opposes such restrictions, an assortment of possibilities can be explored.

Israel is a different matter. On one hand, the progressiveness and egalitarianism of Israeli society rival that of the United States. Women occupy the highest levels of government and most esteemed secular professions. According to a 2012 survey conducted by the Jerusalem-based Guttman Center, more than three-quarters of Israelis self-identify as non-religious, a diverse category encompassing the anti-religious, the holiday observant, and the merely secular. Such identification does not come with the existential crisis so often present among secular American Jews. Since Israel is a Jewish state, asserting one's Jewishness does not require overt displays or the extra effort of synagogue membership. When the majority of the population is Jewish, assertion is unnecessary. This is partly why the Reform and Conservative movements have struggled to capture the popular imagination. (Recent strides in this regard owe much to the efforts of several contributors to this book.)

On the other hand, the state-appointed twin rabbinate in Israel (Ashkenazi and Sephardi) is granted a level and type of power distinct from its counterparts elsewhere in the Jewish world, ancient or modern. As a consequence, Orthodox Judaism is in essence the "established state religion" of Israel, making it exceedingly difficult for other forms of Judaism to find a place within the political structure and in the hearts of the people. Like most subjects touched upon in this introduction, obstacles faced by Israelis seeking more diverse religious expression are too many to enumerate.

Perhaps the most illustrative is the fact that Israel establishes *halakhah* as state law in issues pertaining to personal status, including marriage, divorce and conversion, and gives rabbinic courts the authority of civil courts in these matters. Rabbinical appointments are granted through a complex process involving the Ministry of Religious Affairs, chief rabbinates, local rabbinates, and religious councils, all of which are comprised almost exclusively of Orthodox Jews.[8] Within this religious structure, the leaders of the *haredim* wield enormous influence on public policy. Although their numbers are small (roughly 7 percent of Israelis), they are empowered to implement their interpretation of religious law on the larger population.

This political reality gives Orthodox Judaism the status of an official state religion, and it creates a distance between the Orthodox and the secular majority, many of whom harbor negative feelings about "religion." For most Israelis the idea of women serving as rabbis or cantors is not only contrary to the type of Judaism to which they are exposed, but it is also unappealing. Since women cannot be clergy in the Orthodox system and since that system dominates, even progressive Israelis have difficulty imagining the possibility of Jewish clergywomen. A typical line of questioning might be: "Is it even possible? If so, is it worth it? Why would a woman want to get so involved in religion, anyway?"

The chapters that follow provide enlightening and richly detailed answers to these questions. They are voices in the wilderness: clergywomen sounding forth from the deserts of Israel, confronting religious prejudices, challenging societal norms, and offering much-needed words of clarity, wisdom, hope and promise. Each contributor was trained and/or serves in the Reform movement, largely because of the movement's embrace of women clergy and Israel's historic denial of that possibility. But their stories are much larger than affiliation. Through the inviting lens of personal narratives, they touch upon

an array of contemporary issues and academic disciplines, including
politics, philosophy, feminism, theology, sociology, performance
studies, ethnic studies, and psychology.

In part one, Rabbi Maya Leibovich recounts how a television
interview with Kinneret Shiryon, the first woman rabbi to make
aliyah to Israel, inspired her to become the first Israeli-born
woman to enter the profession, and how she has used her calling to
bring a sense of *kehillah*—Jewish community—to modern-minded
yet spiritually thirsty Israeli Jews. Rabbi Miri Gold tells of her soul
and identity searching journey from Detroit, Michigan to an Israeli
kibbutz, and her landmark case in the Israeli Supreme Court to win
government salaries for non-Orthodox rabbis in the country. Rabbi
Ilana Baird describes her early struggles with Jewish identification
growing up in Soviet Russia, and how her exposure to Shabbat
services at a broken-down synagogue in Chelyabinsk eventually
led her to Israel, where she established a Reform congregation for
young Russian-speaking families in Haifa. Rabbi Gila Caine reflects
on her early childhood and adolescence, when she struggled for a
sense of power and dignity within the confines of male-dominated
Orthodoxy.

In part two, Cantor Meeka Simerly relates her transition
from an ultra-secular Israeli to an intense spiritual awakening, to
immigration to America, to a religious calling, to assuming the pulpit
of a synagogue in Northern California. Cantor Miriam Eskenasy
details her slow road to the cantorate, involving a childhood in a
Zionist Romanian family, upbringing in Israel, teenage years in
Ohio, training in New York and Jerusalem, and her current role as
cantor of Chicago's KAM Isaiah Israel Congregation. Cantor Maria
Dubinsky tells of her search for identity as she moved from Moscow
to Tel Aviv to New York, and the surprising support she received
from her Orthodox parents when she decided to become a cantor.
Cantor Galit Dadoun Cohen describes being raised in an observant
Sephardic family in Israel, being introduced to American Reform
Judaism as a teenager, moving back to Israel, relocating to New York
to pursue a career in opera, and changing course to become a Reform
cantor. Cantor Tamar Heather Havilio explains how her experiences
in theater, prayer and music have inspired her to apply performance

studies to Jewish practice, and to develop innovative approaches to service leading as head of cantorial studies and the prayer development workshop at Hebrew Union College in Jerusalem.

NOTES

1. Ba"had is an acronym for *ba'sees ha'dracha*, meaning "training base." Ba"had Echad translates to "Training Base One."

2. David Golinkin, "'*Kol B'ishah Ervah*'—Is it Really Forbidden for Jewish Men to Listen to Women Singing?" *Responsa in a Moment* 6:2 (2011): 1.

3. The first movement ordained woman in the United States was Sally Priesand (Reform). See "Priesand, Sally J." in *Reform Judaism in America: A Biographical Dictionary and Sourcebook*, ed. Kerry M. Olitsky, Lance J. Sussman, and Malcom H. Stern (Westport, CT: Greenwood, 1993), 168-169. Regina Jonas received private rabbinic ordination in Berlin in 1930, after graduating from the Hochschule für die Wissenschaft des Judentums (College of Jewish Studies), but that was an anomalous incident.

4. The Reform movement instituted cantorial ordination in 2012, changing the terminology from investiture, which had been used since its cantorial school opened in 1948 at the Hebrew Union College-Institute of Religion. The term is applied retroactively to cantors who graduated prior to 2012.

5. There were isolated cases of women serving in cantorial positions prior to their official training and recognition. The earliest known example is Julie Rosewald, who served as "cantor soprano" at Temple Emanu-El in San Francisco from 1884 to 1893. For a detailed account, see Judith S. Pinnolis, "'Cantor Soprano' Julie Rosewald: The Musical Career of a Jewish American 'New Woman,'" *The American Jewish Archives Journal* 62:2 (2010): 1-53. Betty Robbins was the first woman appointed as cantor in the twentieth century. She was hired by Temple Avodah in Oceanside, New York in 1955.

6. Blu Greenberg, "Woman as Messenger of the Congregation: Musings of an Orthodox Jewish Feminist," *Journal of Synagogue Music* 17:1 (July 1987): 10.

7. The latter view is recorded in the *Shulhan Arukh* (OH 75:3). For a more complete analysis of *kol isha* and its ambiguities, see Golinkin, "'*Kol B'ishah Ervah*,'" 1-10.

8. For more ramifications of the power given to the Orthodox rabbinate in Israel, see Louis Isaac Rabbinowitz "Rabbi, Rabbinate: In Israel," in *Encyclopedia Judaica*, 2nd ed., vol. 17 (Detroit: Macmillan Reference, 2007), 18-19.

PART 1

RABBIS

Rabbi Maya Leibovich is the first Israeli-born woman ordained as rabbi by HUC-JIR in Jerusalem. Since her ordination in 1993 she led a congregation of the Reform Movement in Mevasseret Zion which grew from a nucleus of six families to over two hundred family members sharing a home of prayer and an annual cultural educational and religious program. Over the last four years she served as head of the Israeli Reform Rabbinical council (MARAM). Rabbi Leibovich was amongst the first rabbis to go to the Former Soviet Union and teach Reform Judaism. She is married to Menachem Leibovich, vice chairman of KKL-JNF, and has four children.

Maya has published on a variety of topics, including rabbinics, Jewish identity, liturgy, and women's perspectives in Judaism.

1

THE FIRST ISRAELI-BORN WOMAN TO BE ORDAINED

A Personal Story

Maya Leibovich

Background

HOW DID IT ALL START?

"What led you, a longtime teacher and mother of four small children to go back to school and choose the rabbinate as a new direction in life?" This was the most common question I was asked by friends, colleagues and even strangers. In 1993, the year of my ordination, my choice raised many brows.

In 1986 I was watching the news on television when Kinneret Shiryon, the first woman rabbi who made *aliyah* to Israel, was interviewed. The lingual combination of "woman rabbi" was strange to Israeli ears in those days. The thought that a woman could serve as a rabbi never occurred to me. I watched the interview with awe. Kinneret was asked how she would measure the success of her work in Israel and her response was, "When the first Israeli-born woman is ordained." I am fortunate to be that woman. But the story needs to start at the beginning.

I was born to parents who fled Czechoslovakia at the beginning of World War II. Both lost their entire family, homes and memories. My father was a descendant of a wealthy family of eleven brothers and sisters, the Schoens. They owned a large store of construction materials in Prague and lived a comfortable life. They were an Orthodox family, and my father often mentioned his mother's religious observance.

By 1939 my father already had an administrative job in the store and his father Leopold, being sensitive to the changes in Europe and the winds of war, sent him to Palestine to see what the

Zionistic craze was all about. My father was barely settled in this hot, humid, new land when the Nazis conquered Czechoslovakia, and it was no longer possible to escape. Except for one brother, everyone else perished.

My mother came from an enlightened family. She only had one brother. In spite of great objection by her parents, she joined the *aliyat ha'noar* (the youth *aliyah*) movement and came on illegal *aliyah* to Israel. She never forgave her parents for not allowing her to take her brother with her. There were no survivors on her side either.

My parents met in a café in Tel Aviv.

These were the stories I heard at home. But there were other stories I did not hear and I discovered them in strange ways.

In my childhood home, God was not present. My father repeatedly said, "If God could stand by and witness the Holocaust and do nothing then he is no God of mine." Consequently, synagogue was not a place to frequent and during holidays very little Jewish tradition was observed.

I remember missing a sense of belonging to a family. I had no grandparents, no uncles, aunts or cousins. I remember the envy I felt as children came back from school vacations and told stories of visiting with family at a *kibbutz* or *moshav*. I even remember trying to attend synagogue one Yom Kippur. I stayed behind, alone in the women's section of our neighborhood synagogue until half the neighborhood was in search of the missing child. No, I did not reconnect then.

I was in many ways a sapling with no roots. Czechoslovakia and the Holocaust were not a topic to talk about at home, yet both were very present in our lives.

There were few things to remind my parents of the homeland they had fled and even fewer mementos. For example, above my bed in an open closet were photographs, one of my grandmother walking hand in hand with my father on one of their vacations at Karlsbad.

The other photo was of a mother and child. The woman was beautiful and the girl looked much like her. I often asked my father who they were but he brushed me off, blushing, saying they were distant relatives. It was strange, as he spoke freely and at length about the other photograph of my grandmother.

Next to the photos was a little red wooden heart my father gave me as a present. It had a tiny door and when it opened there was a photo of my father as a young gentleman with a blonde curl attached to it. My father said it was a curl taken from my first haircut.

I cherished the little heart very much but also felt strange about the blonde curl. In none of my childhood photos did I seem to be even close to blonde. All fell into place many years later.

One wintry night my father asked me to bring him a pair of socks from the wardrobe in my room. I took a pair out, unfolded them, and out fell a line of contact photos. My father was seen in them clad as a bridegroom and next to him stood the lovely lady from the photograph clad as a bride. I put the contact photos back, slept on it for a fortnight, and then approached my dad with many questions.

The discovery was not only that my father was previously married but also that he had a six-year-old daughter named Marcella. He never said so but I guessed the blonde curl was hers, for in the few photos he had hidden she was definitely blonde. I gained and lost my family simultaneously. I gained new names but none were alive.

It was only when I started my journey back to Judaism that I traveled to Czechoslovakia and went through Terezin and Auschwitz, as well as the Terezin archives at Kibbutz Givat Haim in Israel. This was the beginning of reclaiming my family that was no longer alive. Today I have a family tree and documentation of their last journeys.

I have no good answer to the question of why I chose not to research it all much earlier, or how the rabbinate was connected to the abyss in my family history. The fact is that when I saw Kinneret Shiryon on Israeli television, it felt as though a door of hope had opened for me. It started a journey back home.

Beshert, that same night Kinneret appeared on TV. Menachem, my better half, was being interviewed in Jerusalem by Rabbi Asher Hirsch for the post of C.O. of Beit Shmuel, the Center of Reform Judaism, the construction of which had just begun. At the time we lived in Arad, a small town outside of Beer Sheva and I was already a mother of four small children. When Menachem came back from the interview in Jerusalem, I told him of my newest discovery—women rabbis! Menachem was always my greatest supporter and he, too, was excited by my enthusiasm.

It was a daring step to go back to study with four little children at home. I had many moments of rethinking and regret, but the new "Jewish bookcase" that had opened before me, the *hevruta* with Hebrew Union College (HUC) seminary students, the reconnection to my own tradition—it was all stronger than my second thoughts.

For my family the move from Arad to Jerusalem opened up a new life. We joined the Reform Congregation Harel in Jerusalem and began changing our home to a more religious environment. For my older son, ten at the time, it was challenging and he often revolted while the other three joined quite willingly. My oldest finally reconciled and when asked by anyone what his mother's profession was, he said proudly, "A Reform rabbi!" This candidness frequently led to loud debates on the school bus, and he found himself confronting quite a few of his friends. When I was ordained and he stood by my side, I felt his pride in my achievement.

My other three children were a more integral part of the family's Jewish journey. At a later age each one of them in his/her turn taught trope to bar and bat mitzvah youngsters in my congregation and the synagogue became a second home to each of them.

It is perhaps fate that my husband Menachem was raised by his father in Congregation Harel in Jerusalem. His father was among the founders of this first Israeli Reform congregation in Jerusalem. When we became members of that same congregation, Menachem was also coming home.

Through the rabbinate I reclaimed both my personal family as well as my national family.

Attending synagogue every Friday and returning home to a shared dinner, often with guests, created a new order for the weekends. The topic of discussion around the table wandered to the Torah portion of the week and the sermon Rabbi Tovia Ben Horin had given that night. Add to that the *Kiddush* and singing and our family life was greatly enriched.

Although I was a teacher for many years, I never felt the deep sense of passing on Jewish traditions to the next generation. The rabbinate allowed me to reconnect to the ethos and the narrative of the Jewish people. I know my children now have a choice in their lives to create a Jewish home, an option I was not given by my parents. This fills my heart with gratitude. The rest is history. I was ordained in 1993 as the first *Sabra* (Israeli-born) woman rabbi.

Kehilat Mevasseret Zion

During our final year of studies at HUC in Jerusalem, Naama Kelman (today dean of HUC-JIR's Jerusalem campus) and I were asked to lead Torah lessons and Kabbalat Shabbat for a small group in Mevasseret Zion. There were about seven founding families who met in private homes and shared creative Shabbatot.

At the end of our first year, Naama and I suggested examining the need in town for an egalitarian prayer group. We announced the services for the High Holidays in the local paper. We were taken aback by the response. Over a hundred people attended services in the hall of the school we were using. That was the beginning of Kehilat Mevasseret Zion, a congregation known today as KAMATZ.

As the wisest of men said, "Many rivers flow to the sea but the sea is never full" (Ecclesiastics 1:7).

I have described only one river upon which I sailed back home. There were others no less important. I am not sure that in 1986 I could have fully put them into words. The rabbinate has given me both the understanding as well as the vocabulary.

One river in particular I need to remember: a need for a sense of belonging. In his book *Future Shock*, Alvin Toffler writes about three basic needs every human being experiences: The need to live in a community, the need for a framework for one's life, and the search for meaning.[1] I have discovered all three in congregational life.

Many sociologists and anthropologists agree that being part of a congregation, caring for a family larger than one's immediate family or lone self makes for a healthier life. In his book *Sane Society*, Erich Fromm talks about the difference between antiquity and modern times.[2] He examines man's escape into over-conformity and the danger of robotism in contemporary industrial society. Modern humanity, he maintains, has been alienated from the world of its own creation. He says that today we function in societies that expect us to *sell* ourselves, while the old ideal was *being* yourself. The modern human being has distanced himself from family and often functions in solitude.

Congregational life offered me the gifts of giving and belonging. The claim that no Jew is alone took on a personal meaning for me.

I have since discovered that this deep sense of togetherness is expressed both in the language and customs of Judaism. The Hebrew word for congregation is *kehillah*, from the root *kahal*, a congregated group. However, there is a difference between *kahal* (a random audience) and a *kehillah*. A congregation is a combination of *kahal* (audience) and *yah* (the name of God). Therefore a *kehillah* is a sacred congregation, a group of like-minded people who come together due to their covenant with God.

It is expressed also in Jewish customs. For example, to pray in Judaism is to pray in a group—in a *minyan* (a group of at least ten participants). Even on the holiest day of the year when Jews come before God to ask for repentance we speak in first-person plural language: *ashamnu, bagadnu*...("We have become guilty, we have betrayed..."). Even then we depend on each other; the fate of the world lies on the shoulders of each individual. Rambam says it so beautifully in *Sefer Hamada, hilhot T'shuva*, chapter three, *halacha* 8:

> *One should, accordingly, consider himself as well as all the world half meritorious and half culpable all year long. And [he should believe that] if he were to commit just one sin, he would incline himself and the entire world toward guilt and bring about destruction; and, contrarily, that if he were to fulfill just one mitzvah he would incline himself and the entire world toward merit and bring about salvation and redemption. As it is written: 'A righteous man is the foundation of the world' (Proverbs 10:25), [which is to say that] the righteous themselves incline the world in the direction of merit and rescue it.*

This combination of fate and destiny was probably one of the reasons Jews in the Diaspora always lived in closed circles and in close geographical proximity. It served two basic purposes: (a) they could depend on each other and share the communal services (school, synagogue, bakery, kosher grocery, charitable institutions); and (b) they could observe their religious and cultural way of life without bothering their neighbors. Two basic Jewish values underlined the Jewish community: The covenant between God and Israel and their mutual responsibility to one another.

In the Talmud (Sanhedrin 17b) we already hear of the institutions that constitute this organization called Jewish *kehillah*:

> *A scholar should not reside in a city where the following ten things are not found: A court of justice that imposes flagellation and decrees penalties; a charity fund collected by two and distributed by three; a Synagogue; public baths; a convenience; a circumciser; a surgeon, a notary; slaughterer and a school-master.*

So we can see that the Jewish congregation (*kehillah*) took care of all basic institutions: law, *tzedakah*, education and public services such as medical care, and all the trades.

This creative Jewish organization gave every Jew a sense of belonging to a people of the same ethos, culture, language and traditions. At the same time, it empowered the community and provided channels of communication with the local rulers on behalf of the Jewish community.

Although this structure had its flaws, it remained effective until modern times. With modernity the walls of the Jewish ghetto disintegrated and Jews began traveling to new lands. Secularization and mingling with the general society carried Jews away from what was until then a warm Jewish "home."

Part of my rabbinical mission is to offer *kehillah*—a congregational lifestyle to those who no longer live in a ghetto but experience a sense of alienation and loneliness that typifies the modern industrial era, in which so many responsibilities fall on the shoulders of the individual. I have seen it in my own family as we moved from a small town to a big city, where we felt lost. We found Jewish meaning in Congregation Harel and have been part of a Jewish congregation ever since.

As a rabbi in Israel, I find that the social togetherness, the congregating element, has a vital meaning to Israeli families. They come to celebrate lifecycle events, usually a bar or bat mitzvah.

They attend services and share Shabbat dinner together, during which they discuss the rabbi's sermon. Thus begins a process of reconnecting to Jewish values.

We have to give credit to the Orthodox and ultra-Orthodox communities that never gave up on congregational life. As a Reform rabbi, one of my main goals is to create this greater Jewish family in the town of Mevasseret Zion.

A Better Israel

I did not come to the rabbinate from a feminist stance, but I have learned to appreciate the egalitarianism Reform Judaism offers Israeli society. I shall never forget a youngster who came to register for the bar/bat mitzvah workshop on his own. Neither of his parents accompanied him. When asked, he explained that his father grew up in an Orthodox family. He left religion and did not want his son to practice it, and his mother didn't care. Yet he wanted to celebrate just as his friends did. When I asked him why in a Reform synagogue, he replied without hesitation, "I want my mother by my side." Noam's parents eventually thanked him for teaching them that there are many ways to be Jewish and that by "throwing the baby out with the water," you have a lot to lose. I have met many Noams since.

As a woman, I have to admit I am still touched by every girl who decides to read Torah. It took three or four years before the first bat mitzvah was celebrated in KAMATZ. Today, twenty years later, girls make up about thirty percent of each workshop. In Israeli society it is not common for girls to claim their place in synagogue. Although today many Israelis are aware of the existence of the liberal movements, it is still somewhat of a novelty.

I feel women are agents of change and the growing demand for women to claim their place in all walks of life will certainly continue to increase in Israel. We cannot call ourselves a true democracy while the rights of half of the population are disregarded.

As a rabbi I strive to ensure a better future for the coming generations in Israel. There are many ways to do this. Mine is via offering Israelis a journey through Jewish text, a regaining of an ancient and rich heritage, a meaningful celebration of lifecycle events, a sense of peoplehood and a rich community life within a congregation. To date, we have done quite a lot in our small town of Mevasseret Zion.

For the past four years I have served as chairperson of *Maram*, the Israeli Reform Rabbinical Council. This position allows me to take part in shaping the Israeli Reform rabbinate of the future. I have had the honor of coaching young rabbis, just out of school, and I can say full-heartedly that my homeland of Israel will gain much by the growth of Reform Judaism. As Rabbi Asher Hirsch once said to me, "More than Reform Judaism needs Israel [and he truly believes it cannot exist without Israel], Israel needs Reform Judaism."

On my recent retirement, I looked back and thanked God for coming back into my life, thanked my family for the journey we have taken together back to Jewish communal life, and thanked my congregation for allowing me to be their leader and spiritual guide.

NOTES

1. Alvin Toffler, *Future Shock* (New York: Random House, 1990).
2. Erich Fromm, *The Sane Society* (New York: Rinehart, 1955).

Rabbi Miri Gold was born in Detroit, Michigan, and grew up at the Conservative synagogue Shaarey Zedek, with Rabbi Morris Adler *z"l*, and Rabbi Irwin Groner *z"l*, and Congregation Beth Shalom. At sixteen, Miri went to Israel for the first time and returned for her Junior Year Abroad at Hebrew University 1969-1970. She graduated from the University of Michigan, *cum laude* in 1971, with a degree in Philosophy.

Since 1977, Miri has been a member of Kibbutz Gezer, Israel, serving as the rabbi of Kehilat Birkat Shalom, a regional Reform synagogue located at Gezer. She attended Hebrew Union College in Jerusalem and became the third Reform woman rabbi to be ordained in Israel. At the same time, she received her M.A. from Hebrew University at the Institute for Contemporary Jewry.

Miri petitioned the Israel Supreme Court in 2005 for recognition as the rabbi of Gezer and a salary on par with the sixteen Orthodox rabbis in the Gezer Regional Council. In 2012, the Israel Attorney General decided that the Ministry of Culture pay salaries to rabbis of non-Orthodox councils and farming communities. This decision represents a major step toward religious pluralism in Israel. In 2013, monies were transferred to four Reform, one Conservative, and one Secular rabbi, for "cultural and spiritual activities" in non-Orthodox communities. Rabbi Gold is the first non-Orthodox rabbi to be recognized by the State of Israel. She was named by *The Forward* newspaper as one of the five influential women rabbis in Israel 2010.

She is married to Jewish educator David Leichman and has three children.

2
AN UNFOLDING JOURNEY
Miri Gold

Beginnings

I WAS BORN MARILYN RAE GOLD, FIRST child of Ruben and Lillian Betty Gold. I was also born Miriam Rachel Gold, Kislev 10, 5710, daughter of Reuven, son of Chaya Kroll of Minsk and Shmuel Gold of Pinsk, White Russia, and Leah Bracha, daughter of Haya Malka Axelrod and Baruch Katz (Kohen Tsedek), of, respectively, Koitches (near Parritch and Bubroisk in the Minsk Geberny), and David-Horodok, White Russia. In both cases, my hometown was Detroit, Michigan, but the home of my ancestors was in the more mysterious land of Israel. With parallel American and Jewish identities, I was proud of my dual heritage.

Yet, clearly I was more an American Jew than a Jewish American. While I fondly remember sitting on Santa's lap and touring the neighborhoods in the family car to see the spectacular Christmas lights, my strongest associations are of Jewish holidays, family gatherings with my three younger brothers, many aunts, uncles and first cousins, sitting in *shul* with my grandfathers where they sniffed smelling salts on Yom Kippur during the fast, Saturday morning services at Shaarey Zedek with the lavish *Kiddush* table featuring seven-layer cake, going for the *kichel* at "*shaleshudes*" on Shabbat afternoon (later to be understood as "*seuda shlishit*"), and Pesach, Shavuot and Sukkot at the neighborhood Beth Shalom. The rule was "*shul* or school," and I took off every *shul*-going holiday possible.

My earliest memory of formal religious training was Sunday school at the Labor Zionist Haim Greenberg Center in Detroit. My father dropped me off the first day, after drawing a funny face on the blackboard (when the teacher angrily asked who did that, I was too afraid to answer). The only thing I remember from that time was learning "*Kum bachur atzel, netze la'avodah. . . . Kuku riku kuku riku tarnegol kara.*" ("Get up lazy boy, let's go out to work. . . Cock-a-doodle-doo called the rooster.") Who knew that the roots of the kibbutz were already being planted in my psyche and my fledgling Hebrew vocabulary was being enlarged by "*koo koo ri ku,*" the sound of an Israeli rooster?

Later, my parents brought a teacher to the house to tutor me in reading Hebrew: "*Sha . . . shaw . . . sheh . . . Shalom.*" I went to Shaarey Zedek Religious School in the fourth grade, feeling old and behind everyone else. My mother chose to join that Conservative synagogue, which later was to have a very expensive building fund because of the fine reputation of its after-school program. As I learned later on, my parents had looked into affiliation with the Classical Reform Temple Beth El in Detroit. For my free-spirited mother, it was too different from the *heimish shul* that her grandfather had built upon moving to Detroit. My father was a proud ethical Jew who didn't relate to Jewish rituals or the synagogue on a deep level. Perhaps if, at the time of their marriage in 1949, they had visited Temple Israel, which broke off from Beth El in the late forties, they would have found the right balance for them between ritual warmth and the ideals of prophetic Judaism, and I would have grown up a Reform Jew.

During tenth grade, the girls went through consecration. Conservative synagogues did not have confirmation. Since we were not allowed to "have a bat mitzvah," as we used to say erroneously, we practiced a Shabbat cantata, which had lovely music and introduced me to a melody of *Vayechulu*, which precedes the Friday night *Kiddush* over the wine. My close friend Bonnie sang it solo, giving this liturgy even greater meaning for me as it recalls her lovely voice.

I didn't always take my mother's wise advice. Looking back, I can now admit that she had a good sense of what would bolster my Jewish identity and knowledge, while at the same time opening new opportunities for friendships. One suggestion that I responded to with no hesitation came while I was in after-school religious school. Through my Conservative synagogue, I was entitled to join the United Synagogue Youth Pilgrimage in the summer of 1966, between eleventh and twelfth grade. The only condition, as far as my mother was concerned, was that I continue with Hebrew school and graduate the following year. I agreed. As a conscientious Hadassah lady (so I thought) she wanted me to learn about Israel, and to love and support the country. Of course, neither one of us had any inkling that I would become so smitten that I would eventually make Israel my home.

What did I know about Israel at that point? At Hebrew school, I bought paper leaves to stick on a tree in order to have a tree planted in Israel. I sang *Hatikvah* very solemnly with my favorite teacher, Emil Wolok, who would put his hand on his heart as we all stood and faced the Israeli flag. I knew that my uncle Jerry had spent a year on the first Habonim workshop in 1951. There were various exotic items in my grandparents' home, such as a bottle of colored sand depicting a desert scene, and certificates and plaques showing the pioneers toiling in the field of the Land of Israel.

The seven-week trip to Israel was powerful. My travel diary lists many of the sites we visited, some of which were forgotten until I reread the journal forty-six years later. The most significant memories of that trip include the Shabbat morning visits to diverse synagogues in Jerusalem—Persian, Bucharan, Italian, The Great Synagogue, Yeshurun—where we spent every Shabbat; a visit to the Givat Ram campus of Hebrew University, when several of us casually suggested that we come back to Israel for our junior year abroad; and the few days spent cleaning neglected army trenches on the Castel overlooking the road to Jerusalem. Little did we know then that the following year would bring the Six-Day War, and that those trenches would be used by the Israeli army.

I returned home knowing how to *daven*, since we had prayed three times a day—sometimes on our hotel porch, sometimes on a mountaintop. I learned *Birkat Hamazon*, and began to keep kosher out of the house as well. Prior to that, our family only observed *kashrut* in the home, originally out of respect for my great-grandmother who was part of my life until I was twenty-one. We did not avoid non-kosher foods at restaurants, and my favorite food on the menu of the local Howard Johnsons was a "swanky-franky," a hot dog wrapped in bacon and cheese. My parents, who stayed away from pork and shellfish at all times, did not limit our choices.

I went to Hebrew school enthusiastically, especially enjoying the spoken Hebrew class with a former Miss Israel. As promised, I graduated from Hebrew school at the end of twelfth grade.

At the University of Michigan, I studied Hebrew for two years, and then, as planned, went to Hebrew University of Jerusalem for my junior year abroad, 1969-70. Naively, I aspired to speak fluent Hebrew without an accent. I did learn fairly decent conversational Hebrew, but the accent remained a Midwestern-Eastern-European-Ashkenazi one, which to this day brings peals of laughter from my kids when they ask me to say our phone number—*sheish-shevah-shevah* (6-7-7). It shouldn't be so hard, when there is no *reish*, but it is a lost cause.

That year, 1969-70, was life changing. It was a time when Israelis were patriotic and sincerely believed that they were living in the only safe place for a Jew. Ironically, it was the time of the War of Attrition and the loss of life among soldiers, which was difficult.

Overall being in Israel was exhilarating for me. Living the Jewish calendar from Rosh Hashanah through Shavuot, I was particularly aware that holidays were enhanced by the natural cycle of the seasons. Growing up in Michigan where winter lingers, it was delightful to discover that one could comfortably sit in the *sukkah* for seven days, and that Pesach is indeed the holiday of spring.

I must admit that I was shocked that on Rosh Hashanah people went to the beach, and that synagogue-going was not the norm for non-Orthodox Jews. However, unless someone had their head in the sand, it was impossible not to be embraced by Shabbat and holidays, as the customs, the media, the schools, the cultural events were always focused on celebration and discussion of these special days. How special it was to walk around Jerusalem on Yom Kippur with no cars in sight. Marking the observances of Holocaust Remembrance Day and the Memorial Day for fallen soldiers, as well as Israel's Independence Day, sharpened my knowledge and appreciation for modern Jewish history and for remembrance in a truly visceral way. My Jewish identity was strengthened and my loyalty to the Jewish people deepened. Though I resisted the persistent pleas of my friends to stay in Israel, I was becoming more and more comfortable in the rhythm of life there.

During the year in Israel, I volunteered to help a young Yemenite girl, Tziona, with her English. I retained ties with her family, and was invited to her wedding after I had already moved permanently to Israel. I remember her mother and her nineteen siblings saying "*b'karov etzlech*," wishing me to find a husband in the near future. The relationship with the family taught me that giving to others brings rewards. I received love and attention from the family and that was very precious to me, especially because I very much missed my family at home. Tziona's mother, who at the time had "only" sixteen children, would treat me to chicken soup with *hawaj*, a special mixture of spices. I was always grateful to feel that I was like another beloved child in the family. While they were of very modest means, they rolled out the royal carpet for me.

During that year, I wrestled with the question of living in Israel. I had never felt threatened as a Jew in the United States, and I had no difficulty being an observant Conservative Jew, in spite of attending public schools.

Had the availability of Jewish day schools been more common, I would liked (in hindsight) to have been able to attend one. However, during my school years, my mother wanted her children to be good Americans and be part of the public school system. In her later years, she probably would have thought differently. I remember that when we moved from Detroit to the suburbs as I was entering fifth grade, I asked my mother what she thought about the idea of changing my name legally from Marilyn to Miriam, and she objected. Perhaps this opinion reflected the fact that she was one of a few Jews to attend nursing school at the University of Michigan in the late 1930s. Perhaps she was sensitive to the anti-Semitism when her father worked at the assembly plant of the Ford Motor Company. He was physically attacked by his co-workers, and was left with a broken back and a very long recovery. Perhaps it was my parents' pride in being Americans. They always flew the American flag on national holidays, and both of my parents were veterans of World War II; my mother an army nurse and lieutenant, my father the recipient of a Bronze Star for his service with the Army Air Corps in Guam.

Only when there were conflicts of interest did I realize that the United States is essentially a Christian country. Important student events like the Michigan vs. Michigan State football game could be scheduled on Yom Kippur in complete disregard of Jewish life. Paul McCartney and Wings concert could be scheduled on Purim, which meant that Jewish students who wanted to go to the synagogue to hear the Megillah could not go to the concert.

The hardest thing for me to imagine was being away from my beloved family. During the year, however, I realized that, as an adult, I would not necessarily live close to my immediate and extended family. I decided not to worry about it, thinking that if and when I would decide to make my home in Israel, I would have worked out this sensitive issue.

By the beginning of my senior year at the University of Michigan, I was already homesick for Israel. I did not know when I would move to Israel, nor did I have any idea where I would live or what I would do. With a bachelor's degree in philosophy and the ability to type, I had no direction. By that point my command of the language was good. I knew that I felt at home in Israel. For some reason, I did not want to label myself a Zionist or anything else. When asked why I wanted to leave the United States and move to Israel, I would quip that my children would not have to go to Hebrew School. Truly it meant that they would know Hebrew as their native tongue, and they would study the Bible, Jewish history and geography and be "assimilated" into a Jewish country.

Moving Toward Aliyah—Onwards and Upwards

I joined an Israel interest group and met a Habonim *shaliach* (emissary) who was trying to put together a group to make *aliyah* and formed an "urban" kibbutz in an abandoned Arab village near the Lebanese border. Though that never materialized, a weekend spent at Camp Tavor changed my life forever. I met the people with whom I would form a *garin* that eventually made *aliyah* to Kibbutz Gezer in 1976, through the Labor Zionist Habonim Youth movement. Upon graduating from college with a degree in philosophy, I worked at the Israel Aliyah Center, from which I processed my own *aliyah* documents. In 1973, I spent a month in Israel celebrating the country's twenty-fifth anniversary. Afterward, I thought about traveling and then eventually moving to Israel. In the immediate aftermath of the Yom Kippur War, I went to Israel as a volunteer at Kibbutz Grofit, a place I had actually visited in 1966. All plans for world travel went by the wayside, and for a while I was involved in forming a *garin* to Grofit.

When I graduated from college in 1971, I called Rabbi Groner at Shaarey Zedek to ask if I could be called to the Torah as a bat mitzvah. I had asked when I was twelve and was turned down. I had hoped that synagogue policy would have changed almost a decade later, but I was disappointed again. It didn't occur to me to search for another way to fulfill this wish. Fittingly, I had an opportunity to speak as a rabbi from the *bimah* years later, with Rabbi Groner beaming beside me, proud of my accomplishments.

My last year in the States was spent in St. Paul, Minnesota, a wonderful Jewish community and a wholesome and enjoyable American city. I was becoming more observant, and stopped traveling on Shabbat. I would frequent the local Conservative synagogue, but for one of the holidays, I was invited by the Chabad rabbi and his family for dinner. I remember being frustrated that such an invitation was not extended by anyone in the more liberal Jewish community. Perhaps that is why my husband David and I are constantly hosting people for Shabbat and holidays. I worked at the United Jewish Fund and Council as the executive assistant to the director, Morrie Lapidus. During that year, I was exposed to the educational materials and lectures sponsored by the Jewish Federation. I remember being convinced that it was important to have more than 2.2 children, to break the trend of zero population growth and to "replace" some of the Jews lost in the Holocaust. I donated a hefty portion of my salary to the Federation for the Israel campaign.

In the end, I decided to go to Gezer with twenty people, including some friends I knew from my experience working at Camp Tavor. Some of them remain among my most precious friends. *Aliyah* to Gezer was a milestone in my life's journey, primarily because I met my future partner-in-life, David Leichman. A native New Yorker, we found that we shared many things in common, and together we still strive to live a life of values based on our Jewish heritage. I have learned a great deal from his world-outlook, his humor, and his abilities as a Jewish educator. Often he has challenged and encouraged me to be an active leader when my natural tendency would be to shy away from the spotlight. We have been blessed with three wonderful children.

Part of my decision to rejoin the *garin*, which I had helped to found, was based on the fact that Gezer would be a liberal Jewish religious community, which would have a kosher kitchen and a creative Jewish lifestyle that would combine our backgrounds as Reform and Conservative Jews with the innovative culture of kibbutz holiday celebrations. During our six-month *hachsharah* (training period) at Kibbutz Tsora, we understood more clearly why we wanted to create a unique community. There they had a great Purim party, but didn't read the Megillah. On Friday evenings, there was no *bet knesset*, and candles were lit without a blessing. On Pesach, they used the Kibbutz Movement Haggadah, full of lovely songs and celebration of the springtime, but with no mention of God.

In addition, after my two volunteer stints at Grofit, I realized that I didn't want to be different from the majority. I had had enough of that in the States. The kibbutz was willing to accommodate me with a kosher corner in the kitchen, but I would have been one of very few who were interested in a synagogue, which was non-existent there. I also felt alienated from mainstream Israel on other issues, especially those dealing with women's equality. At Grofit, women were not allowed on tractors due to the contention that it would ruin their uterus. At Tzora, women worked shorter hours on the assumption that they were the main caregivers for their children. Feminism was dismissed as promoting bra burners.

Gezer was meant to be different. There was a synagogue space in the old one-room classroom. We planned Kabbalat Shabbat and holidays to reflect our observances in the U.S. The public spaces were kosher. Women had equal opportunities at work, and there was no definition of "women's work." However, men who did not want to do a rotation in the children's houses were not pressured or cajoled as were the women.

The reality was that we were so busy running "the farm" that our declared interest in liberal Jewish practice, ecology and liberal politics took a back seat to the immediacies of the day. Our library was full of our old college texts from the humanities and social sciences, as well as books about civil rights, women's history, and Vietnam, but there was not one book about plumbing, electricity, carpentry, dairy farming or anything else technical. My informal love of cooking, baking and being a "*yiddishe mama*," who served meals to my friends, landed me in the kitchen where I worked for ten years, eventually taking a cooking course, and then doing the meal planning, purchasing and budgeting. My initial desire to be a translator did not materialize into a reasonable income contribution to the kibbutz, and thus was never pursued.

While I held various managerial and committee chair positions on the kibbutz, I was not initially active in creating our Jewish holiday celebrations. Eventually, many of us felt frustrated. Jewish life was taking the back burner. True, we enjoyed the cultural Judaism offered by the country, and we did have some wonderful and innovative celebrations, but we never had an easy time with Kabbalat Shabbat in the dining room. The Friday night meals were special, the basic blessings were said, but there was no satisfying cultural program preceding the meal as was customary on more established kibbutzim. We were struggling to fulfill our initial dreams about being an active Jewish community.

After we had children, who would eat for five minutes and then run outside to play with all the others, we decided to have Shabbat dinner at home so that we could recreate the special experiences we had growing up with our families.

In 1979, with our frustration growing, someone suggested that we invite Professor Moshe Davis from the Institute for Contemporary Jewry at Hebrew University for a weekend to help us move ahead. He used the kibbutz model to suggest that, just as we had committee chairs and work branch coordinators, we needed to relate to our Judaism in the same way. We decided to write to a friend, Levi Kelman, who was about to complete rabbinic school at the Jewish Theological Seminary, to spend a few months with us. We enticed him saying that, instead of turning a synagogue into a community, he could take an existing community and turn us on to synagogue life.

Levi stayed for four years, becoming a member, and working in the dairy, the children's house, and in the kitchen. He volunteered to take care of the synagogue and started a tradition of Kabbalat Shabbat services in an old one-room classroom that had a Torah scroll and some prayer books, but no chairs or sense of decorum. We would leave our shoes at the door to keep the place clean (there was a great deal of mud at the time due to lack of proper sidewalks), sit on mats, and do some hatha yoga followed by a few songs. Eventually we had a booklet of prayers, but we were always careful to finish in time to make it to the communal Shabbat meal in the kibbutz dining room. For those of us who chose to go to the synagogue, it meant a major adjustment. It was one of our customs to host or visit families on the kibbutz before Shabbat dinner. In deciding to go to synagogue services, we were making a conscious decision to forego the pre-dinner visiting hour, something that previously had been done regularly.

When Levi left to spend a year with Rabbi Hugo Gryn in London, things fell apart. There were no Kabbalat Shabbat services at all. For High Holidays we would coax a few of our members to lead services, and then tried bringing in rabbinic students. It was never satisfactory. A woman friend of mine, from a nearby kibbutz, learned of an opportunity to study to lead High Holiday services. I joined her, going to Jerusalem with a tape recorder and reviewing the services, much of which were familiar to me from childhood. In addition, I renewed the Kabbalat Shabbat tradition in the synagogue, because I felt so dismayed that nothing was happening. Did I make *aliyah* to become less observant?

Rabbi-To-Be

I took on a "para-rabbinic" role, learning how to lead services for Friday nights, High Holidays, and Passover *seders*. When the oldest kibbutz children became bar and bat mitzvah age, the alarm went off and the red lights flashed. The oldest boys went to the ultra-Orthodox kibbutz down the road, and the very first bat mitzvah-age girls schlepped to Jerusalem to study for their *aliyah l'Torah*. I found this unacceptable. We came to Gezer to create a liberal Jewish lifestyle, and when we succeeded in celebrating together, it was meaningful and satisfying. Just as we decided that our kosher kitchen would function without an Orthodox *mashgiach*, so too did we want our customs and ceremonies to be based on our liberal (Reform and Conservative) backgrounds, and at the same time borrow from contemporary Israeli cultural Judaism.

I began to teach trope to the bar/bat mitzvah kids, after I refreshed the skills I had learned on the kibbutz. Levi Weiman-Kelman, today the rabbi of Kehilat Kol Haneshama, prepared me for my first *aliyah l'Torah*, which consisted of a Haftorah reading. I was thirty-one with a one year-old baby daughter in my arms. Later, during 1990 to 1991, I learned Torah cantillation with the help of Cantor Nancy Abramson, now director of the Cantorial School and College of Music at the Jewish Theological Seminary in New York, who was then on a sabbatical at Gezer. I remember that my first student was one of the girls on the kibbutz, and as I tried to record her lines, I found myself trembling and nervous. By the time my daughter was twelve, I was more confident, and helped her prepare for the ceremony in 1993. I also read from the Torah, in the presence of my two rabbi mentors, Levi Weiman-Kelman and his sister Naama Kelman, today the dean of the Israel campus of Hebrew Union College. They, along with my mother Lillian and my husband, David Leichman, convinced me to explore rabbinical school. I received permission from the kibbutz, and was excited about the possibility of serving the community of Gezer.

My family had spent two and a half years in Boston, from December 1986 to July 1989, when David was a *shaliach* on behalf of the kibbutz movement and the Reform movement. Since both of us had grown up in Conservative homes, Reform synagogues and summer camps were a new world. We weathered the First Intifada in America, discovering that many of our Jewish acquaintances were fair-weather friends when it came to Israel. David formed "Zionists Anonymous" so that we could discuss Israel critically without being called self-hating Jews. Our daughter went to the Solomon Schechter School and our son went to a Hebrew-speaking nursery school. We missed Israel. Just before we returned to the kibbutz at the end of the *shlichut*, our youngest child was born.

I decided not to return to the kitchen right away, and was elected chair of the Absorption Committee. The *mazkirah* (mayor) at the time was a social worker by profession and suggested that I attend a seminar for people looking for second careers. I was forty and had no idea what I wanted to do. I took a test that showed that I was suitable to be a social worker or a pastor. The young man who created the test as part of his graduate studies laughed with me at that possibility. It never occurred to either of us that pastor might mean rabbi.

In 1994, at the age of forty-four, with three children ranging in age from thirteen to five years old, I began my studies at the Hebrew Union College (HUC) in Jerusalem. I had considered studying at Schechter, the Conservative movement seminary in Israel. I chose not to apply there because the Masorti movement (the Conservative movement in Israel) was not as egalitarian as I had hoped. Women were not counted as witnesses, were not part of the *minyan* in every congregation, and congregants were encouraged to walk to synagogue.

My experience with the Reform movement in Israel was a comfortable fit for my religious practice. It reminded me of the liberal Conservative atmosphere with which I identified, and was quite different from the little contact I had with the American Reform movement. Studying at HUC required a master's degree at a university, and this also attracted me. I chose the Institute for Contemporary Jewry at Hebrew University, and concentrated on American Jewry as my field of study. At every opportunity, I would study and write about the American Reform Jewish experience. To my delight, I enjoyed discovering the history, ideologies and theologies of modern Reform Judaism. My master's thesis explored the phenomenon of traditional Jews from Europe who became part of the Reform movement in America, which was already established in the U.S. for many years. This came out of a personal curiosity, because I could not imagine my traditionally Jewish grandparents joining a Reform temple. I discovered that there were different circumstances that brought Eastern European immigrants to the Reform movement. It was not an ideological issue. Some immigrants found themselves living in communities, particularly in the Midwest and West Coast, where the only synagogue in town was Reform. Others married Reform Jews. Others saw Reform affiliation as a ticket to becoming more Americanized and accepted.

As a child, my Reform friends were unfamiliar with the synagogue, the Hebrew language, holiday rituals, and Jewish history. To call someone "very Reform" meant that they knew very little. Today, I consider myself a Reform Jew with pride. My thesis for HUC looked at Reform rabbis who were Zionist before the 1937 Columbus Platform, which was the turnaround moment when the Reform movement declared itself Zionist. Looking at Stephen S. Wise, Judah Magnes and Abba Hillel Silver, I learned that all three of them came from traditional European and Zionist backgrounds. My Zionist roots came from my maternal grandparents, and while I had considered them Orthodox in their practice, they were actually very open to the modern world.

Ordination

I continued to lead services on the kibbutz and to officiate at bar and bat mitzvah ceremonies for kibbutz members as well as people from the neighboring communities. In 1997, partway through my studies, Kehilat Birkat Shalom became affiliated with the Reform movement as a regional congregation. In 1999 I was the third woman to be ordained as a Reform rabbi in Israel, and the first female kibbutznik to do so. I followed in the footsteps of Naamah Kelman and Maya Leibovich, as did Ada Zavidov, who was ordained minutes after me. Birkat Shalom became a recognized not-for-profit organization, and I started to receive a third-time salaried position from the Reform movement in Israel.

Understandably there was a great flurry of press coverage. One headline was "cute," calling me "Rav Cookie" as a takeoff on the Rav Kook, because I love to bake and at the time I began my rabbinic studies I sold chocolate chip cookies on behalf of the kibbutz to an ice cream parlor. Another was annoying, titled "Rebbetzin in Jeans." On a morning television show, the interviewer, who before the broadcast told me that she sometimes attends the Reform synagogue in Tel Aviv, said, "You know they hate you, don't you?"

Early on a wise friend told me not to read the comments online underneath the various articles. I decided that whenever possible I would be a bridge-builder, and resist lashing back at the hurtful and stupid comments.

I understood that many Israelis had never heard of a woman rabbi, and often had misplaced prejudices about Reform Judaism. On the few occasions that a young couple asked me to perform their wedding (not officially recognized by the State of Israel), there was always the danger that they would sheepishly return to tell me that some relative couldn't handle the idea of a woman rabbi officiating. My own children kept silent about their mother's new profession because they didn't know how to explain what it meant to be a woman rabbi.

Upon ordination, I formally became the rabbi of Kehilat Birkat Shalom at Kibbutz Gezer, a regional Reform synagogue dedicated to providing religious services and a spiritual home for Jews living in the surrounding area. Today the congregation has about seventy member units from the kibbutz, the region, and surrounding cities.

One of the first steps I took as a newly ordained rabbi was to join Rabbis for Human Rights, of which I am currently a board member. One of the founders, Rabbi David Forman *z"l*, was a close friend from my junior year abroad experience in Jerusalem. It has always been important to me to work towards civil and human rights, and to promote a peaceful solution between Jews and Palestinians. One year I went olive picking in the West Bank, a place I otherwise do not visit, and was chagrined by the fact that the Arab family we were helping couldn't believe that we were volunteering to help them. As much as I love Israel and defend its sovereignty (and have experienced what it is like for my children to put their lives on the line for its survival), I fight for its ethical and moral character as well, internally and externally. I admire the philosophy of Viktor Frankl, who, in keeping with Jewish philosophy, advocated that, no matter what the circumstances in which we find ourselves, we have the ability to define our attitudes and choose our course of action. Writing on love and the ability to bring out the highest potential in those with whom we are closest, he said:

> *Love is the only way to grasp another human being in the innermost core of his personality. No one can become fully aware of the very essence of another human being unless he loves him. By his love he is enabled to see the essential traits and features in the beloved person; and even more, he sees that which is potential in him, which is not yet actualized but yet ought to be actualized. Furthermore, by his love, the loving person enables the beloved person to actualize these potentialities. By making him aware of what he can be and of what he should become, he makes these potentialities come true.*[1]

At the end of 1999, I was part of a three-person team of educators sent to Romania for a seminar involving young adults. I was told by the organizers that I was not to reveal that I was a rabbi, since everything in the community was done in an Orthodox fashion. In some ways it was amusing to see young men wearing *kippot*, *davening* with a separation (*mechitzah*) from the women, and then to see them pile ham on their plates for breakfast at the hotel. Believing in "live and let live," I did not want to criticize their choices, but I was disturbed that the leadership was Orthodox in its thinking. Informally I did let it be known that I was a rabbi, and many of the young people were impressed and supportive. At the request of several women, I led an introductory session about chanting Torah with trope.

While being a woman rabbi definitely comes with more hurdles than those faced by male colleagues, it was discouraging to realize that many Israelis had very negative views of the Reform movement. They so dismissed us that it didn't matter who held what position, male or female. In a meeting I attended of the Knesset Education Committee, an ultra-Orthodox man stomped out of the meeting when he realized that he was in the presence of Reform Jews. On the other hand, an eleventh-grader attending the meeting as part of his civics class made a point of saying that he had the right to be given educational materials about the Reform and Conservative movements so that he would be able to make choices for himself as an informed person.

People challenged me, asking if I drove on Shabbat, kept kosher, or allowed people to smoke in my home on Shabbat. I did drive every day, but I kept kosher, and never allowed anyone on any day to smoke in my home. I understood that the only way they could ask questions was to put it in an Orthodox frame of reference. Most of the people asking were "secular," but assumed that the Orthodox way was the only right way. I contend that Judaism is not black and white, that there is a spectrum of choice for Jewish identity and observance.

Of course there were others who were happy to learn that Reform Judaism fostered equal opportunities for women in the realm of prayer services and rituals. Though at first I hesitated to tell people that I was a Reform rabbi because I feared being verbally attacked, I gradually became more comfortable. As long as someone treated me respectfully, I had no difficulty if they disagreed with my position. Even so, I came to understand the limits on religious pluralism in Israel and the place for more tolerance and respect of different traditions of Jewish practice.

"The Miri Gold Case"

In 2005, the Israel Religious Action Center, the legal arm of the Reform movement in Israel, approached me about becoming a plaintiff in a Supreme Court case demanding that Reform and Conservative rabbis be eligible to serve their communities. It took seven years before the Attorney General of Israel announced that rabbis of non-Orthodox communities were entitled to receive salaries from the State, through the Ministry of Culture and Sport.

During that long and seemingly endless period, more and more Israelis were becoming familiar with Reform Judaism. A reporter, who appreciated the importance of democracy in Israel, commented after one of our court appearances that it was a case of "taxation without representation." When people would ask me if I was discouraged, I would say that hope is a *mitzvah*, a commandment, and that hope is what drove us to keep actively pursuing our goal of strengthening Israel as a democracy. The Declaration of Independence in 1948 clearly stated that there must be freedom of religion in Israel. In these modern times we are fighting for freedom from the Orthodox rabbinic institutions, which so often dictate to the State of Israel in the areas of lifecycle events and daily practice. It was only during the third court appearance that the president of the Supreme Court, Dorit Beinisch, asked if there was really a Miri Gold. I stood up and said "I'm alive and breathing," meaning alive and well. I realized that what was important was not the particular plaintiff (myself), but rather the principle that a healthy Israel must have a functioning democracy that upholds the ideals promoted by the vision of the prophets and the founders of the modern State of Israel.

As for my role, I would often cite the case of Alice Miller, who won a Supreme Court case in Israel allowing her, a female, to try out to be a pilot in the Israel Air Force. While she did not become an Air Force pilot, she paved the way for other women. Today there are women pilots and navigators. I hoped that "The Miri Gold Case" would open the doors for liberal rabbis to serve their communities, with the same rights and privileges as Orthodox rabbis. In my area, the Gezer Regional Council, there are sixteen Orthodox rabbis serving the twenty-plus communities in the region. Kibbutz Gezer has very little formal contact with the Orthodox rabbi who receives a salary for his assignment to serve the kibbutz. As long as the government continued to allocate funds for their salaries, it seemed only just that Reform and Conservative rabbis have that option as well.

Lech Lecha—Leave Your Father's Home

While suffering through various bureaucratic and political obstacles and numerous court appearances, life went on. In 2008, I was invited to Bensberg, Germany to speak in various forums. I was invited by a Protestant church group I had met through my involvement in Rabbis for Human Rights. This was not an easy decision for me at first. Having grown up in a home in which German-made products were noticeably absent, I had never wanted to visit Germany. I thought it would be too painful a reminder of the Holocaust. However, as I contemplated the trip, which would fall on the Shabbat of *Lech Lecha* and Kristallnacht, I realized that I too was making a new journey. Having met German volunteers at the kibbutz and through my contacts with members of the

Bensberg community, I readily answered that I would be honored to come to Germany. Had I not become a rabbi in Israel, I don't know that I would have had this special opportunity to explore and change my own prejudices.

On the plane ride to Cologne I noticed that the city had a chocolate factory. When asked by my hosts what I would like to do, I said I would like to see the famous cathedral and visit the chocolate factory. My polite hosts agreed, but first it was important for them to expose me to the painful reminders of Nazi Germany. They took me to the Gestapo headquarters and to the Jewish school yard where children had been rounded up for deportation. Prior to my departure for Germany, I had read an article about a Jewish boy who had been cautioned by a German policeman to run home for safety on the eve of Kristallnacht. That boy eventually moved to Israel. As an army commander during the Kafar Kassem incident when Arabs were shot if they were not in their homes by curfew, he instructed his men to allow people to get home safely.

The Journey Continues

I felt very privileged that my role as a rabbi has allowed me to experience and explore the world. I remember being shocked that people related to me differently because of my title. I learned to realize that I had taken on a public responsibility, to be the most moral and ethical person I could be, and that I had the ability to influence others. As a role model of female leadership, I was encouraging people, especially women, to find their own assertive voice, to champion the causes important to them. It is said that every rabbi has a theme that they teach over and over again. My mantra is that every human being is created in the image of God, and that we must look for the divine spark in every encounter. With this belief, it is important to me that we get to know the "other" and shed our fears, to celebrate our differences as much as we find comfort in being with like-minded people. I promote tolerance, religious pluralism, and freedom of religious expression in Israel. It is hard to know when and where I might have a positive influence on others, especially when the religious conditions in Israel are so confrontational.

Not long ago, my younger son told me that at a local pub he met a group of young women, all in their early twenties, who were very impressed that he is the son of Miri Gold. Apparently they had been part of a bar/bat mitzvah group from Karme Yosef, a community in the Gezer region, who participated in a program held in the Jewish educational park of Pinat Shorashim at Gezer. I led part of the session, in which we fully opened a Torah scroll. They came and they left and I had no further contact with them. Their parents were not part of Birkat Shalom, but had decided to offer them a supplemental Jewish educational experience as part of their seventh grade bar/bat mitzvah year at school. Now, about seven years later, parallel to the time it took for the Supreme Court case to yield its fruits, they were shaking his hand and expressing their admiration for his rabbi mother.

On May 29, 2012, my younger son's birthday, Attorney General Yehuda Weinstein made the pronouncement that "rabbis of non-Orthodox communities are entitled to receive a salary from the government of Israel." It was decided that funding would come from the Ministry of Culture and Sport, for fifteen Reform and Conservative positions in regional councils. This gave hope that the Supreme Court case from 2007, advocating that rabbis in city neighborhoods could also be Reform and Conservative, would also be won. In the heady days after this historic precedent, we already looked ahead to a time when our Reform conversions and weddings would be recognized by the State.

Not long after this, the Minister of Culture and Sport, Limor Livnat, apparently asked to delay implementation of the decision. As of the end of 2013, we are still in the process of proving that we fit the requirements set by the Ministry. The Israel Religious Action Center (IRAC) is continuing to carry this case forward to a victory on the ground. It is uncertain whether the monies to be received will even cover the half-time salary of $2,000 a month that I currently earn. But no matter what, eventually there will be more funds to help the Reform and Conservative movements in Israel grow and be strengthened, to offer their liberal Jewish services to a greater number of Israelis who are looking for alternative ways to celebrate their Judaism in Israel.

I am currently involved in raising money for a modest new building for our congregation. This is a result of a previous Supreme Court case won by IRAC, stating that government monies have to help Reform and Conservative congregations acquire buildings, just as the government has traditionally helped Orthodox communities. The court has clearly declared that there are, *de facto*, streams of Judaism existing in Israel, and that they must be recognized. Unfortunately, the political parties in the Knesset are only now starting to cautiously address the issue. The director of the Israel Movement for Progressive Judaism (the Reform movement), Rabbi and lawyer Gilad Kariv, ran for a spot within the Labor Party, on the platform of religious freedom. While he didn't get a promised slot in the election, he did succeed in gaining cooperation and support from other Labor Party Knesset members to address these issues. This is progress in the right direction.

Modest achievements are still achievements, and we can build on these advancements and successes. Personally, I am proud to be part of the mission to create an excellent Israel. In making *aliyah*, it wasn't enough just to move to Israel, but rather to help create a better society. I had no idea at the time that I would have a defined role. I was not seeking it. I am grateful for the opportunity to be part of a team effort to gain recognition for Reform and Conservative rabbis in Israel, as a way to strengthen our place as liberal Jews in Israeli society. This in turn will hopefully help strengthen the bonds between Israel and Diaspora Jewish communities. To me, it is of utmost importance to foster a love of Israel, out of which we can be constructively critical when necessary. As I recently heard, "Cement, and then Dissent!" Together we work to assure a lasting relationship among Jews the world over. Hopefully we can help achieve a just and compassionate Israel for all its inhabitants. When we work together, we can make a significant impact.

The Ba'al Shem Tov illustrated the power of community: "From every human being there rises a light that reaches straight to heaven. And when two souls that are destined to be together find each other, their streams of light flow together, and a single brighter light goes forth from their united being." So, too, when the communities of Israel, worldwide, band together, we can bring forth the light of which our prophets spoke.

Being a Reform woman rabbi in Israel is always challenging. I never expected to be in a managerial position in my synagogue. I never expected to find confrontation and disdain for my liberal Jewish beliefs. I thought it would be easier to be Jewish in Israel, that I would have a better chance of having Jewish grandchildren. Today I understand that the world is a very complex place and that there are no simple solutions to sustaining the Jewish People. I feel blessed and honored that my journey is still unfolding, and will continue to step up and step forward to do my part for Judaism, for women's rights, for peace between people and among neighbors. If in some humble way I might inspire others to act, to lead, to make a difference, my journey will be all the richer.

NOTE

1. Viktor Frankl, *Man's Search for Meaning: An Introduction to Logotherapy* (Boston: Beacon Press, 1992), 116.

Rabbi Ilana Baird lives and works in Silicon Valley in Northern California. She is a community leader of the Russian-speaking Jewish community. She works at the Jewish Community Center in Los Gatos planning, promoting and leading Russian language programming in various communities and congregations. Outside her work at the JCC, she works in Russian language programs throughout the San Francisco Bay Area. Previously, she established a congregation for young Russian speaking Jewish families in Haifa, Israel, Shirat HaYam-Carmel, part of the Israel Movement for Progressive Judaism.

Ilana was ordained at the Hebrew Union College in Jerusalem in 2006. She earned her undergraduate degrees and an M.A. in Jewish history at Haifa University. During her rabbinic studies, Ilana traveled to Russia, Belarus, Ukraine, Latvia and Germany to support local communities in Jewish education, leading High Holidays and communal programs. Ilana has led programs at Jewish camps in the FSU and in California.

Before living in California, Rabbi Ilana Baird lived in Israel, after making Aliyah in 1993 from Chelyabinsk, Russia. In Haifa, Israel, she married and had twin daughters who recently celebrated their B'not Mitzvah.

3
ILANA'S LIFE
Ilana Baird

AN OLD CALENDAR HUNG ON THE DARK, CRACKED WALL. On the back was written a Russian phonetic transliteration of the Jewish prayer, *Lecha Dodi*, a *piyyut* sung on the Jewish Sabbath. This is how my Jewish-conscious life began. It was winter, Friday night, in the abandoned building of the old synagogue of the city of Chelyabinsk, Russia. It is the same city that was recently hit by a large exploding meteor. The large industrial city in the Urals was closed to foreigners at the time. Factories and plants could be found everywhere in the city, and produced tanks and tractors. Nuclear research and development occurred around the city, as well.

A Jewish Upbringing in Soviet Russia

My maternal great-grandparents, the Meilakhs, came to the Ural region in Russia for various reasons. They came in the early twentieth century. They arrived in Chelyabinsk in 1912 from Dvinsk, Latvia. My maternal great-grandfather, Abraham Meilakh, came seeking to expand his business. Pre-revolution Abraham was a merchant of the wealthy first guild. Jewish merchants in the Pale, the western regions of the Russian Empire, were required to be members of the first guild for ten years before being allowed to settle in the Russian interior. My maternal grandmother was born in a *shtetl* in Borisov, Belarus. She was born to a large Jewish family that one day left their home after an epidemic disease took two of their children just before the Great Patriotic War, known in the west as World War II. My grandmother and her family gathered up their few worldly possessions and traveled from their hungry town to the cold city of Chelyabinsk.

The relatives on the paternal side of my family were also Jewish, but many were killed during World War II. My paternal grandfather Rabinowitz, was a soldier in the armored corps during the war, and my grandmother was from a Jewish family in the Ukraine.

To My Own Terrible Dismay,
All My Ancestors Were Jewish

The first time I heard that I was a Jew was in kindergarten. The teacher instructed us children to ask our parents about our nationality. I did not quite understand why. The next day, all the other children smartly replied that they were Russian. When I replied that I was a Jew, I learned the harshness of that word. I was the only one who answered that question with the word "Jew." That day, I learned I was not a Russian. I asked my mother again and again the reason for my difference. For the first time, I felt uncomfortable with my own identity. All my school life, I would have to carefully avoid the entry in my passport: "Jew." I wanted to figure out how to change my pure Jewish name, Rabinowitz. The name is used to refer to "Jew" in all the Jewish jokes. Problems associated with my Jewish heritage haunted me everywhere—in school, during after school activities, and so on.

All I knew about Judaism was that it was bad, uncomfortable and even embarrassing. My grandparents sometimes inserted phrases in Yiddish into their speech, which seemed to me to be a terribly vulgar jargon. They would listen to old records, which I did not understand. Once a year, in the spring, a special bread called matzo appeared on our table. I did not know why it should have been there, but my grandmother said that Jews were supposed to eat it—and I ate.

In high school, I moved to a new school and did not record my nationality in the class register. My teacher did not say anything. I suspected that she, too, had Jewish roots and changed her name when she married. Later in life my suspicions were confirmed. I had the best two years of my life, and realized that it was because I had hidden my nationality and identity.

The Synagogue of Chelyabinsk

My hometown of Chelyabinsk was not in the Russia of Tevye the Milkman, familiar to all of us in the film *Fiddler on the Roof*. The first Jews to settle in the Urals were Jewish soldiers conscripted from the Pale who had served in the imperial army for twenty-five years and did not change their faith.

Toward the end of the nineteenth century, the Jewish population of the city greatly increased. Jews concentrated mainly near the city center, on Masterovaya Street. On that street lived a merchant of the second guild, Brent Solomon. In 1884 he bought a plot of land at 6 Masterovaya Street specifically for the construction of a synagogue. The new synagogue construction began in 1903 and ended in 1905. It was built of brick and was 400 square meters on two floors, with a prayer hall and a balcony covered with iron. The Star of David affixed to the thick walls would never be destroyed throughout the subsequent Soviet regime.

When the synagogue opened, it had a Jewish school, funeral society, and society to support poor Jews. Before the October Revolution there was an active Jewish community. During the First World War, the synagogue also served as a small military hospital, which cared for Jews and non-Jews. After the Revolution, in 1919, Hebrew books were banned along with the study of the Hebrew language. Religion was removed from the state, and the Jewish school was closed. In 1921, all the silver of the synagogue was confiscated, and in 1929 the Bolshevik government declared the synagogue closed. For many years afterwards, the building ceased to fulfill its true destiny. In the 1930s, the synagogue was turned into a concert hall, and in 1937 it became an orthopedics factory. The building was no longer in good repair, and its layout had changed. An additional floor was built for the factory warehouses, workshops, and machinery. The street on which the synagogue stood changed names, and aside from an obscured Star of David, it was no longer recognizable. The city of Chelyabinsk had become a closed city in the Soviet Empire, hidden from the rest of the word. The Jews, along with their old synagogue and the rest of the city, were unknown, forgotten, and tried to forget their Jewishness.

In 1992, after a long list of owners, the synagogue on Pushkin Street, Building 6B, was returned to the Jewish community by the new Russian government. I was a witness to the transfer of a part of the building to the Jews of Chelyabinsk. The building's state of repair was worse than a barn: windows and arched spans were laying around, floors had fallen or were near collapse, and much of the building was full of rats. In the dilapidated synagogue where, besides the exterior walls, nothing was left whole, a Jewish community attempted to perform prayers and celebrate the holidays. To this synagogue came the first Jewish guests from abroad.

A Renewed Jewish Life

In this broken-down synagogue begins my own magical journey to discover my Judaism. My mom found a group of people gathered in that old building and decided that we, too, had to be there with the Jews who wanted to renew Jewish life. On Saturdays in the synagogue elderly Jews gathered for prayer and formed a *minyan*. Somehow, they still remembered the prayers of generations past. We, the young Jews of Chelyabinsk, gathered on Friday night, brought a guitar, lit candles, and had a good time. We, the young ones, got to know each other, and celebrated holidays as best we could. Then, on one of those Shabbats, I saw a calendar on the wall with the words of *L'cha Dodi* in Russian transliteration. There were a lot of people in the synagogue, many whom I did not know. I was told that guests had arrived from abroad. Guests from abroad to the "closed" city of Chelyabinsk?

Changes were occurring very rapidly in the Former Soviet Union. Shortly before these events, in 1991, was the first time I saw someone in Chelyabinsk who arrived from Israel! He was singer and composer Uzi Hitman, bless his memory. An incredible number of Jews had accumulated in one of the large concert halls of the city. I knew a few Jewish people through my mother, but I had never seen that many at one time. At the concert there were hundreds of people I'd never met, and surely they were all Jewish. At that moment I realized that I had never been alone, and never would be.

In the synagogue that Friday night was the second time I met people from Israel in Chelyabinsk. There was a woman and there was a man. I was told that one was from America and the other from Israel. Another rumor was that one of them was a rabbi. I clearly remember that night, but the details are foggy. Candles were burning, it was very cold outside. It was also cold inside the synagogue, but my heart was warm and happy. I felt that we were part of something big, very big—part of an ancient people who lived in different parts of the globe.

Suddenly, everything changed magically. I found that being a Jew was not shameful, but rather a matter of pride. My involvement in the Jewish community led to the fascinating world of Jewish summer camps, where for the first time in my life I felt proud to be a Jew. In the morning we said, "*Boker tov*, Israel." I was surrounded by others like me: young Jewish teens. Many wore a chain with a Star of David around their necks and kept wearing them even after camp ended. Some of my friends got in trouble with anti-Semites because of them. Such troubles no longer mattered. We had discovered a wonderful new world of Jewish peoplehood. We were all fascinated and excited to belong to the ancient Jewish people.

I found the meaning of life and was feeling special. I absorbed whatever Jewish knowledge I could find. I took on some Jewish traditions. I decided for myself to try to comply with some of the rules of *kashrut*. I gave up sausages and frankfurters, and anything that might contain pork. I started to keep track of what I ate. I tried to separate dairy from meat at home. I did all these things not because I read the Torah and thought about the interpretation—"do not boil a kid in its mother's milk"— but simply because other Jews had done so before me. Keeping kosher brought me closer to my great-great-grandmothers and to my people. My Jewish identity emerged as I started to think about and enact Jewish traditions.

Since then, I have lit candles every Shabbat, and always recall that in lighting them, I am reunited with my people, my history and ancient customs.

My mother helped the community. She was a volunteer secretary. By that time, my parents had divorced, and I lived with my mother in a one-bedroom apartment.

The following summer I again went to the Jewish camp of the Jewish Agency, this time as a counselor. I recruited a group of children from Chelyabinsk, and I spoke with dozens of worried Jewish mothers. After the camp, I was invited to Moscow for a training seminar to work as a counselor in other Jewish camps. The seminar was called "Bar Giora."

I was eighteen years old. It was 1993. My grandparents were about to make *aliyah* to Israel. My grandfather was very ill and they felt they could get better medical care in Israel. My mother and I still remained in Russia. In my apartment, the phone rang and I answered. Someone spoke in Russian, but with an Israeli accent. The man said that I was among forty teens who were selected to go and study at a seminar in Israel. I remember my reaction: I was sitting in the hallway, talking on the phone, desperately trying to convince the speaker that perhaps he meant someone else and that it was a random error, a misunderstanding. He repeated my name and told me what I needed to prepare for the passport and travel documents. My joy knew no bounds. I was going to a seminar in Israel. Happiness! A whole month in Israel!

We went everywhere, from north to south. The month of May in Israel is just wonderful. Everything is green, everything is blooming, the sea is blue, the sky is blue, the sun—so gentle! I came back home, dreaming only of one thing: how to quickly get away from the cold, gray mud of Chelyabinsk. Israel was my country. Zionism was my destiny.

Aliyah

In August of 1993, after working at a Jewish summer camp, my mother and I collected our bags and left for Israel. My mother came to Israel tired and exhausted. The process of leaving was not easy, but we finally arrived at our long-awaited destination by the sea, in Haifa, and to my grandparents who were waiting for us. It was very hard. At first we lived in a small room in a hostel for new immigrants. Toilet and kitchen facilities were shared by everyone living on the same floor. We were four people to a room. At night we made up a mattress on the floor for my mother and me. The door opened inward. In order to go to the bathroom at night, my grandparents had to wake my mother and me to push the mattress aside and open the door. My grandfather was robbed because he was afraid to put money in the bank. He had remembered what happened to all his savings in the Soviet Union, which he had lost because of hyperinflation. A month later, we found an apartment for rent in a basement. It was raw and needed repair, but my mom and I would have our own room. We were very happy. We lived in *our* country. We would have to learn the language. We could eat yogurt. Why is it that yogurt made such a great impression on us? In Russia, in the early 1990s, we saw almost nothing in the shops. In Israel, the stores were always full. I was happy and in love with this country—this land in the southern sun. I wanted to know as much as possible about it. So, I decided to apply to the Department of History of the Land of Israel at Haifa University. At first it was hard. It had been only one year since I came to Israel, and I was already starting university classes. In the first lecture on the History of Zionism, I only wrote what the professor wrote on the blackboard. I cried, not understanding ninety percent of his words. I had to ask the other students for their notes and I translated them word for word.

As a student, I met a young man who went along with my mom to learn Hebrew. David was a new immigrant from California. He came to Israel alone. We quickly found a common language and a common interest in Judaism. He was also once a counselor at Jewish summer camps in the United States. We decided to build a Jewish family together.

After I graduated, I wanted to learn more about my people, history and traditions than I had learned at university. I signed up for any additional courses I could find. One day I came across an announcement for a course for community leaders for Russian-speaking Jews. The course was held in the Reform synagogue, Or Hadash, not far from my home in Haifa. We went there on holidays. I gladly signed up for the course. There, I met with Rabbi Moti Rotem and a Russian-speaking student at the Reform Hebrew Union College (HUC), Alona Lisitsa.

Rabbi Rotem suggested that I try to enter the Israeli program at HUC in Jerusalem and train to be a rabbi. I had some experience teaching Judaism. I had good skills communicating and relating with people. I loved to talk about Judaism. I discovered my Jewish identity on my own, and wanted to spread my love for Judaism to other Russian-speaking Jews like myself, who had not yet reconnected to their roots. Still, it was a difficult decision for me, but my husband David supported me. For him, it was very clear and familiar: a woman could be a rabbi. I had already passed through the interviews and taken entrance exams for HUC. During the last exam I felt queasy, and came home absolutely sick. A doctor found that I was pregnant with twins. I also got a call that I successfully passed the exam and that I was admitted to study at HUC. I was ready to give up studying, but was told that I would be able to begin my studies at a time that was convenient for me.

Hebrew Union College

After giving birth to twin girls, and after three months of sitting at home, I had the great pleasure of getting away for one day a week to study in Jerusalem. I needed something to occupy my mind, intellect and spirit while I was a new mother with twins. I gladly engaged in rabbinic studies at the college, as well as a masters degree program at Haifa University. This is how five years of rabbinic studies at HUC began.

As a rabbinic student, I was able to take advantage of my knowledge of the Russian language. I became part of a Russian-speaking rabbinic student program that supported the Jewish communities in the Former Soviet Union (FSU). There were, in fact, Jewish congregations throughout the FSU, but there was a shortage of rabbis. We traveled to the FSU several times, from one community to another. I spent the holidays with local Jewish leaders, and taught leadership training seminars to help them support their congregations. I visited Chelyabinsk among other cities in Russia. I visited Minsk, Mogilev and Bobruisk in Belarus, Kiev in Ukraine, Riga in Latvia, and more.

During the High Holidays, I was invited to a very special congregation in the city of Hamelin, Germany where Russian Jews had settled. There I led services and taught Judaism to newly converted Germans and Russian Jewish immigrants, each with an eagerness I recognized in myself to absorb their newly discovered Jewish identities.

When I would visit a congregation, I worked with the children, adults, teenagers and retirees. Working with all elements of a Jewish community was a valuable lesson for me as a young student rabbi.

As I worked more and more as a student rabbi in Jewish communities in Israel and the FSU, I learned not only how strange it was for many people to meet a female rabbi, but also the hostility of some towards my chosen life path. I saw my rabbinic work and my presence as an opportunity to educate people that times had changed since pre-revolution Russia. I wanted to educate the young children that a rabbi was no longer required to wear a black cloak, felt hat, or keep a long beard.

A New Congregation in Haifa

I had a dream to build a Russian-speaking congregation for young adults and families in Haifa, my home. I didn't really know where to begin. An opportunity came to me, perhaps from above. I was asked to recruit a group of young Russian-speaking Jews for a study group sponsored by the department of Jewish Peoplehood at Oranim College. It was a difficult task, since twenty-five to thirty-five-year-olds were busy with work, studies, and starting new families. All I had to offer was Judaism. A group did come together, and we started our journey through Jewish texts.

One of the members of the group had a baby girl and asked me to do a baby naming ceremony for her. Slowly, people started to ask about celebrating Jewish holidays, since they didn't have friends or family to celebrate with and didn't know how. We held Passover *seders*, *Tu B'Shvat seders* and *Shavuot* study. I hosted *Sukkot* and *Kabbalat Shabbat* at our home. Eventually, the group became interested in starting a Russian-speaking congregation. We formed a board and approached the Reform movement, which accepted us as a new congregation, Shirat HaYam-Carmel.

This is how the only Reform Russian-speaking Jewish congregation in Israel was founded. I am very proud that this congregation continues to function, even after I left with my family to live in California. I now have a new dream to ignite the passion of Judaism in Russian-speaking Jews I have met in my new home.

A Revelation

Several years ago, I was invited to a World Union of Progressive Judaism conference in Moscow. The conference opened with a speech by one of my Israeli teachers and mentors, Rabbi Maya Leibovich of Mevaseret Tsiyon. She began her speech by saying that this was her second visit to Russia. She had previously been in Russia in the early 1990s. She remembered being in the Aeroflot plane, which was beastly, cold and very scary. They came to the distant cold city of Chelyabinsk where she was taken to what she saw as a distraught, run-down synagogue. However, after arriving she met a lot of young people, who were searching for their lost Jewish roots. Singing was a good way to communicate, so she dictated the words of *L'cha Dodi* to someone who wrote the transliteration on an old Russian calendar that hung on the wall for all to see the words and sing. After lighting the candles, her mind was warmed from meeting so many different people who came to the old synagogue, and she hoped that she could bring something of Judaism to them.

After her speech, I walked up to her in a state of amazement. Tears were in my eyes. "Maya, now I know who came to Chelyabinsk." Those Shabbat candles ignited a spark of Judaism in me that has been burning ever since.

Rabbi Gila Caine is a graduate of HUC-JIR's Israeli rabbinic program (2011), as well as HUC-JIR's / Blaustein Center's "Mazorim" Spiritual counseling program (2011). Caine is a graduate of the Hebrew University, with an M.A. in Contemporary Judaism (2009) and a B.A. in Sociology and Anthropology. She has worked as a pulpit rabbi for a number of years (Kehillat Tzur-Hadassah, Kehillat Brit Olam) - teaching, leading Shabbat and Holiday services, counseling and conducting Life-Cycle ceremonies.

She has, and is, also deeply involved in promoting spiritual healing towards and after birth. Teaching and working with women and couples, as well as with professionals (doulas and midwives) - empowering women (and men) in their birth choices, as well as reflecting and healing after difficult birth experiences. As of today (2014), Rabbi Caine is working as a freelance rabbi in the town of Binyamina-Giv'at Ada and its vicinity.

4
ON CREATING A COVEN OF RABBIS
Gila Caine

[Shimon ben Shatah] had vowed that when he would become a Nasi, he would kill all the witches . . . and there are eighty witches in a cave in Ashkelon who destroy the world . . . it was a rainy day. He took with him eighty young men dressed in clean clothes and put them into eighty new pots. He said to them: When I whistle put your clean clothes on. When I whistle a second time, come in. . . . Entering the Ashkelon cave, he said to them "Oyum, Oyum," open up, for I am one of you. When he went inside, one of [the witches] uttered a spell and brought forth bread. Another uttered a spell and brought forth a cooked meal. A third uttered a spell and brought forth wine. They said to him: "And what can you do?" He said: "I can whistle twice and bring forth eighty young men dressed in clean clothes to delight you." They said: "These we desire." As he whistled, they put on their clean suits. When he whistled again, they all entered as one. He signalled to them, each to take one witch and lift her off the ground so that her actions would fail. He said to the one who brought forth bread: "Bring bread," but she could not. And he said: "Crucify her. [To the next] Bring a cooked dish," but she could not. And he said: "Crucify her." So he did to them all. This is why we read in the Mishnah: "He hung eighty women, and one does not hang two in one day" (Talmud Yerushalmi, Hagiga 11b).[1]

Raba said: If the righteous desired it, they could [by living a life of absolute purity] be creators, for it is written, "But your iniquities have distinguished between, etc." . . . R. Hanina and R. Oshaia spent every Sabbath eve in studying the Book of Creation, by means of which they created a third-grown calf and ate it (Talmud Bavli, Sanhedrin 65b).

BOTH OF THE ABOVE STORIES TELL us a great deal about how power is worked in the world, and of the unending ability of men and women to create their own reality and bring their dreams and desires into being. Both of these stories hold secrets of religious and mystical potency and describe the way our spirit self and our body are actually an intricate work of art: our soul working in the world through our flesh, our flesh connecting to holiness through our soul. These women and men, witches in a cave and rabbis studying secrets of Torah, are my spiritual ancestors. I love all of their stories, I study their teachings and I grew up with their words and power in my head. The only problem is that the witches end up dead.

Witches and Rabbis

Remarking on this legend of the eighty witches, Rabbi Orna Pilz explained that the witches are a mirror image to the *Eshet Chayil* (Woman of Valor) whose praise is sung around traditional Shabbat tables. The Superwoman from the Book of Proverbs (chapter 31) rules her house and home, provides for her husband and children, working hard and almost never sleeping. She is so different from the witches who can provide for themselves by speech alone and with little hard work. *Eshet Chayil* has power, but it all lies within the walls of her house, and those who praise her in the end are her children and husband. This isn't a small thing at all, but her song of praise will not accept that she has power over the world of the spirit, or even of the human public world. She's like so many of the women I grew up around, in my modern Orthodox home, who had good secular jobs but sat behind a curtain in the women's section at *shul*.

Can *Eshet Chayil* allow herself to be like those eighty witches, so powerful as to actually be considered dangerous by her enemies?

For me, being a female liberal rabbi in Israel today is about allowing myself to have power. This was, and in many ways still is, a difficult thing for me to learn.

Power and authority; facing society and facing tradition. We all know now what happened to those eighty witches in the cave.

I talked with my five-year-old daughter yesterday about her wish to fly. She told me "I can't fly *yet*, I'm still practicing." We spoke about our gift as humans of creating a reality for ourselves with our minds, of how our soul can fly and we can weave structures of words, actions, and flesh to make all of our reality happen. I know this is why I became a rabbi, to make sure all of our souls are taught this freedom of flight.

Growing up in 1980s and 90s Jerusalem, in a modern Orthodox home, I learned rather quickly what it feels like to have my soul tied down. I'll describe how it's done to young girls. (The method of breaking young boys is different, and I would recommend talking to men who've gone through the process, in order to receive a first-hand testimony.)

By age eight, I remember being ashamed of having a man see me in trousers. I remember being taught to mumble my prayers, like Hannah my lips moving but my voice silent. The method was to make sure no one hears you, but still have your teacher see that you are saying the words.

These two memories are not just in my mind. They are burnt into my body—my limbs and my lips and my flesh. This is why I know that healing is not only about myself, but also about the Jewish people. We must work through our flesh, our blood, the way we touch others and ourselves. We have to re-sanctify our bodily presence in the world.

The description of ways Orthodoxy creates religiously tame young women can be lengthy, and it's all been written about before. These are stories of people who, after growing up, look back and realize they had experienced some form of oppression. It's important for me to know this today in order to understand the source of all the fury and rage I directed toward my Jewish beliefs by the time I was a bat mitzvah—rage that sat for years at the pit of my stomach and weighed down on my heart. I couldn't stand the God of the Jews, and was looking for a way out.

Around that time, I realized my parents' Orthodox synagogue was not the place for me. Entering to pray one Shabbat morning I suddenly understood that from then on I'd be praying from behind the curtain of the women's section. I'm not sure what the trigger was, but I started crying, crying anger and hate at what seemed like being banished, sent into a *galut*. I ran out of that little house of worship and ran home crying and, I think, heartbroken.

It's been almost twenty-five years since that Shabbat, and I've hardly ever gone back to pray in a place that divides people from people. It's not a kosher setting in my eyes.

But where do you go if you are a young religious creature, living in Jerusalem, just a few years before the Internet appeared? How could I worship now? How could I feed my soul?

Not just the synagogue was closed before me. I felt like the whole world of Torah was spitting me out, disgusted or aroused by me, a young female. The self-loathing of a modern Orthodox woman is quite an elaborate construct. You "enjoy" misogynist input on both a religious and a secular level. You play the game of hide and seek not just with the men around you but also with that Über Man: God. I had to find something different, something that would help me find a new way to connect with God—a way that would make me feel part of the conversation, and not just a spectator behind a curtain. And, although during most of the day I would still go out with my friends and do teenage stuff, in all things religious, I took myself into a cave.

Cave

Caves have so many layers of meaning in our spiritual world. We *could* ask ourselves why those witches in the Yerushalmi were meeting in a cave. Caves are a place of wonder and mystical learning—like they were for Rashbi and his son (*Talmud Bavli*, Shabat 33b), a place of deep prayer like they were for King David (Ps. 142), or a place for meeting God when he went to speak to Elijah (1 Kings 19: 10-11).

My other spiritual roots tell me caves are gates to the otherworld, the womb/vulva of our Mother Goddess Earth. You learn all sorts of secrets inside a cave, and in my own private cave I read every bit of myth I could find, and I could find quite a lot! From reading the mythology I also learned about ritual. This was a sort of secret initiation process I was taking myself through, following the words of dead or faraway people to create some sort of path, some form of alternative to synagogue, and a sort of spiritual connection to the world around me.

In a big way, it was also teaching me about the ability to create ritual. This remains for me the strongest thing I've learned: we are creatures of ceremony and ritual, and these tools help many of us make sense of the world around us. As a teenager at my parents' house I would help clear the Shabbat table and secretly (was it really a secret to my family?) go into the garden and pour out libations of leftover *Kiddush* wine to the moon/Artemis/Selena (depending on who I was worshiping that month). I realized I didn't actually need a *minyan*—all I needed was an understanding of ritual and practice with a language that was flexible and powerful, so that the only thing that could stop it would be lack of use.

More than anything else, I think I was learning about power and ways of using it, ways of playing with the elements around me—what do I like burning when I'm sad, when does water work and when do words help me? I would go in and out of my little cave. In many ways this was a split existence. Inside I had knowledge of secrets and creativity, I was a little witch or priestess. Outside the cave I went to my Orthodox girls' high school, and met with my friends and wore skirts and fasted on Yom Kippur and prayed from a *siddur* every morning.

I was building a split in my life—a split between my inside belief and outside expression of belief, and between what I wanted to do with my body and mind, and the way in which I presented it to society. This split has taken years to heal. Maybe it is healing only now, after years on the rabbinic path. Mostly it's healing after accepting that true power is in truth, and that doing the work of God/dess in the world should be with other people, not all by myself.

So the downside of the process was that, while I was learning to find power in the world and some ways of using it in prayer, I had lost the ability to worship out in the open. I wasn't afraid of talking to God/dess, but was insecure about my ability to bring this knowledge to other people, or even just relaxing and praying with them. I had come to equate spiritual satisfaction with loneliness. That wasn't a good place for me to be in. I'm thinking of the myth of the great demon goddess Lilith, how she ran away from silly immature Adam, how she lived the rest of eternity with the demons in the waves. I think that more than anything else, she now teaches me about loneliness, and about wielding great control over life and death and ecstasy, but from hidden and dark rooms. Lilith is a sign for me of true and good power being afraid to manifest itself in the sunlight.

Sometimes doing work on your own is just hiding, sometimes you need to take shelter because it's stormy outside or because there are people out to get you. The witches in the Yerushalmi were in a cave because they knew outside was not safe, outside was where fear resided and the rain poured and Shimon ben Shatah was going to crucify them.

My question was how do I get to be so self-assured, as to be able to sit like Rabbi Hanina and Rabbi Oshaia, creating a calf every Friday and devouring my creation? Out in the open, sure that I could do this trick again when needed, sure that no one would kill or hurt me.

Reading about the gods and goddesses of ancient times, combined with reading any feminist piece of writing I could find, led me to the modern goddess, Mother Earth, guardian of all things female and woman. I was in love with her. I understood that brave women were doing great work of resurrecting and strengthening the female spirit of the world. The strongest ritual I met at the time was a Self-Blessing ritual, as suggested by Z. E. Budapest.[2] In it, you bless your body, part after part from the legs upwards. It was so lovely and quiet and strong. In some places a ritual like this could be the most obvious thing to do, especially today with our Facebook and Women's Circles, etc.; but back then in Jerusalem of the early 1990s this was a revelation for me. It was a revolution. It was proof that religion could actually be an empowering thing for women, that there are real paths for me to talk to God/dess in a contemporary way and in a language that I would actually want to use. That my body and soul were both amazing blessings and gifts.

Creating My Calf in Full Daylight

It's really a question of coming out, isn't it? How do I go about saying things like: I want to decide *halakhah*; I want to speak the language of creative and radical *halakhah*; I want religious authority so that women have a say in Jewish tradition; I want to radically change my own religious tradition because I love it and want it to continue into the future, in the land of Israel, reconnecting to the God/dess of my land who is also a God/dess of the world?

When I decided to return to my Jewish heritage, I knew that the return would be in order to reform my religious culture in a deep way. Having religious power in Israel is not only about bringing women into the synagogue. I'm living in a Jewish state that hardly separates its religious life from its secular life, for good and for bad. So religion and Jewish life are not only about our private and intimate moments, but also about our public life: the way we give birth in hospitals, celebrate, educate our children, take care of our ill and wounded, wage our wars and bury our dead. It's about how we leave behind a minority mentality and take on responsibility, and how we, as a nation, learn compassion and want to live again—not just "not die."

When I was in high school, a good friend of my mother used to sleep over at our house once a week. She was studying to become a rabbi at the Conservative Beit Midrash Shechter. This was at the back of my mind for years, and I cataloged it as a possible solution to where I wanted to take my life.

A large part of my feeling of sadness when I was younger was what I called earlier a feeling of *galut*—of being thrown into a diaspora. I felt I was being thrown away from Torah and all its beauty, which even back then was lovely in my eyes.

When I was in the army, and for the first time in my life living an everyday life with "secular" Israelis, I understood much of their feelings of estrangement from Jewish tradition as a sort of *galut*. Orthodoxy's control over our religious lives has turned Jewish religious practice (and even identity in some cases) into a "foreign land" for many Israelis. It is a place your grandparents came from, and where you visit when you are married or buried. But it is not part of your everyday life.

This was another split I felt should and could be remedied. After all, how can we live as private people and as a nation without our souls?

So, I chose to become a rabbi not only because I love learning and teaching Jewish thought and texts, or because I love praying with people. I decided to join the ancient rabbinic path in order to move some religious power and authority into my own hands, and to have the tools to help heal what needs healing in myself and in the society in which I live. This is about freedom and the ability to create a new reality, like the two rabbis who created a calf for themselves every Friday afternoon. It is scary to take religious power into my own hands, and the responsibility for wielding that power. It opens me up and makes me vulnerable to criticism, self-doubt, and the fear of harming the religious path I strive for. But it is part of the job.

When I was thirty, I embarked upon four years of rabbinic study and growth at the Hebrew Union College in Jerusalem. My mind and soul were being fed in the most amazing ways. During those years as a rabbinic student I also gave birth to my daughter. It was without doubt the best combination of events that could have taken place for me. I felt I was learning secrets of being a scholar and of being a mother, all at once! My mind was expanding and so were my body and sexuality, and womanhood, which made my mind expand to even more remote places.

I had to re-learn the importance of community, and ask questions about the different types of community that exist around me. I had to learn to point at what I wanted and then create it (still learning this one), like Rabbi Oshaia wanting a yummy calf meal every Friday, or like the witches not fearing to say "Yes, bring those young men into our cave, this will please us greatly."

I think, though, that my biggest lesson was learning how to pray and worship with other people again. Letting myself be religious in a social setting was not an easy process for me, but has been a great work of healing, and of learning about power in a group—power that can actually be strong without being violent, like the misogynist synagogues of my childhood.

This hurt sometimes. For long periods of time I wasn't sure if I wanted to be in my house or in my *beit midrash*. I didn't know then that they would both become one place, and that I would learn (and am still learning) to bring them together inside myself.

I'm not forgetting the Goddess and her teachings. She taught me to open up my eyes, as a rabbi, and look at where people feel at home in the deepest sense. Her teachings reminded me that for at least half of the Jewish people, religion was hardly ever in the synagogue or *beit midrash*. She led me to question the importance (or lack thereof) of this structure for a large majority of Jews living in Israel. Could a modern Israeli rabbi really hide herself inside a *beit knesset*? Non-Orthodox Jews in Israel hardly ever go there. We can meet Jews in the park next to our house and at the shops.

Many Israeli Jews are lacking a Jewish spiritual place that can go beyond some of the formal structures defined as "Judaism". While we live inside a huge outer shell called the "Jewish State, many of us are looking for a way to connect, via our Jewish and Hebrew languages, to the spirit and soul of the land we live in and to the everyday needs of our own bodies and souls.

So, I left the synagogue I had worked at for the two years after my ordination, and I'm looking for ways to meet with people inside their own organic communities— families, schools, birthing wards, outdoor festivals. I'm working with teenagers towards their bar/bat mitzvah without asking them to join a synagogue, without imagining that any *minyan* of people could be better than the *minyan* created by their own family.

I'm developing a way of working with women and couples during pregnancy and after birth, so that we don't leave this enormous life event without a good, liberal, Jewish Israeli reference. This is one of my greatest passions: bringing myself as a rabbi into birth, showing that the power of God/dess is manifest through all acts of conception, pregnancy and labor, and discovering and teaching that *Adonai* is a Goddess of life.

Both of the *midrashim* I started with talk about the question of who holds power in the world. Like money, it's often considered impolite to talk about wanting power, to talk about "wanting" in an active sense. This aversion does make sense: we can see a terrible example of abuse of power in Rabbi Shimon ben Shatah's tricks.

But, the text in *Bavli Sanhedrin* tells us "If the righteous desired it, they could [by living a life of absolute purity] be creators." What is a life of absolute purity? And why do you need to be absolutely pure in order to create?

I think being absolutely pure in this case is something like clear water. A person whose mind and body know what they want and where and how to find it. And they do so in clear sunlight and with their *minyan* of friends and family. And with truth and goodwill and courage.

Being a rabbi and, for that matter, being a witch, is about knowing the spells, the words and text, the theory of creation and tradition and ceremony. It's about connecting yourself with very deep roots to the past and the future, to the heavens and to the earth.

Understanding this, and with lots of conviction and faith, you learn how to move reality, how to create meaningful moments of passage in people's and in our nation's life. And hopefully help to create a bountiful existence for all of us here on Earth.

After writing this article about the experience of Israeli clergywomen, I noticed that most of it refers to my earlier years of adolescence, and less is about my "official" progression toward becoming a rabbi. I feel I am trying to integrate (at least) two spiritual paths I've been walking for the last twenty-odd years, and that at this point in time and in my life, I'm attempting to build a joint language for both of them. It feels like *tikkun*.

NOTES

1. Translation from: Tal Ilan, *Silencing the Queen: The Literary Histories of Shelamzion and Other Jewish Women* (Tubingen, Germany: Mohr Siebeck, 2006), 216-17.

2. Z. E. Budapest, "Self-Blessing Ritual," in C.P. Christ & J. Plaskow, eds., *Womanspirit Rising: A Feminist Reader in Religion* (Harper, San Francisco: Harper, 1992), 269-72.

PART 2

CANTORS

Cantor Meeka Simerly was born in Haifa, Israel, and was raised in an ultra-secular Zionist environment. After moving to the United States in 1995 she discovered her Jewish religious roots, becoming musically active in several congregations and Jewish organizations in Silicon Valley. She earned her B.A. *cum laude* in music education from San Jose State University in 2004, and received her Cantorial Ordination and a Masters in Jewish Sacred Music from the Academy for Jewish Religion, California in 2009. She was recently accepted to the rabbinic program at her alma mater, where she will continue her studies toward becoming a rabbi.

Cantor Simerly has served as the Cantor of Temple Emanu-El of San Jose since 2006. In addition to providing spiritual worship experiences for Temple congregants, Cantor Simerly officiates at life cycle events, and shares the love of Torah and sacred text-study with children and adults of all ages. Her essay, "Naomi Shemer's Artistic Expression: Poetry, Prayer, or Both?" was published in *Emotions in Jewish Music: Personal and Scholarly Reflections* (University Press of America, 2012).

In the wider community, she has served as the officiating clergy representative at San Jose's Memorial Day and Veterans Day events. She also works with the Correctional Institutions Chaplaincy, volunteering her time with the Santa Clara County correctional facilities, and was recently invited to serve on the Board of Jewish Family Services of Silicon Valley. She lives in San Jose with her husband and their three Schnauzers.

5

AL KANFEI NESHARIM

On Eagles' Wings

Meeka Simerly

Part One: Sh'ma Yisrael!
Listen Israel to One Woman's Voice

I AM AN ISRAELI WOMAN, A SABRA, born and raised in an Ashkenazi neighborhood of Neve-Sha'anan in Haifa, the only 1970s "hippie" in an otherwise right-wing, Zionist, "ultra-secular" world. When I was thirty, I was living in Tel Aviv, performing as the lead singer of a folk-rock band in the evenings and working at a day job in a record store. During that time I experienced a bizarre vision, and in the following days I had a dramatic car crash, which left me upside down in my car smashed against a fence. Soon after that experience, I felt compelled by an unseen force to leave my homeland to relocate in the land of my dreams, the United States, where I rediscovered my hidden (or stolen) Jewish roots. After years of study in this, my new world, I am now a cantor, an ordained Jewish Reform clergy woman.

I was born in 1965 as Michal Levin, the first daughter of Rivka Chassid and Yitzhak Levin, the elder sister of Amit and Merav. I am half Ashkenazi Russian: my father was born in Palestine, his parents made *aliyah* from Russia in the late 1930s from Russia. Their languages: Yiddish, Russian and Hebrew. I am half Sephardic: my mother's parents were born in Turkey, they brought my mom to Palestine when she was one week old by train, stopping at Rosh Ha'Nikra (the grottos, a northern coastal point in Israel). Their languages: Ladino and broken Hebrew. I am now Cantor Meeka Simerly, married to Dave Simerly. My languages: Hebrew and English. I am a very proud Israeli-American who has lived in the United States since 1995.

Unlike many Jewish-Israeli men and women, I have always known that I belong here in America. I grew up listening to the radio, inhaling every English word and learning to speak it by asking my father to translate songs for me. My journey is different—mainly because I grew up and lived in Israel most of my life, and the minute I landed in America I knew I was "home." Don't get me wrong: once an Israeli, always an Israeli. I love, support and defend Israel with all my soul and heart. But I belong in America.

I love my Israeli heritage, and take pride in my very high-level Hebrew language skills. The fact that I served in the Israeli Army (Sh"alat Yachid, in a kibbutz, a division of the Na"chal), am the granddaughter of Holocaust survivors, and the daughter of an assertive mother and a "macho Israeli" father has opened many doors for me to become the clergy woman I am today: assertive and soft at the same time. It took me over thirty years of walking in a "Desert of Oblivion" (I do not have many fond memories of my childhood growing up in Israel). I was a disturbed teenager, and I lived an unsatisfying life in my 20s.

But, looking back, it was all worth it. I love the life that I created for myself and I don't regret anything I did or didn't do. All of my experiences comprise the sum total of who I have become, and who I am working to become.

First Vision: An Apparition and *Sh'ma Yisrael*

At the age of about thirteen or fourteen, while sitting with my mother in our kitchen and having a pleasant conversation about this and that, all of a sudden, behind her, an image appeared out of nowhere. It was a shadow of a man wearing a Chasid's hat. He was just standing there, with his face turned sideways, just "being." He had a beard, but I could not see his eyes. Blinking my eyes a few times to make sure I was looking at what I was actually seeing, I started staring. I was afraid to say anything. I didn't want my mom to think I was going even crazier than I already felt at that time in my life (just the usual hormonal angsts that teenagers go through). I knew he came to see me, and I knew there was a purpose for that apparition—but I couldn't figure it out!

I went to bed that night immersed in thought, trying to process what it was all about. The next morning I awoke at a very early hour. Half asleep, I reached out for a sharpie, and without even thinking I wrote on the wall behind my head the following words: "*Sh'ma Yisrael Adonai Eloheinu Adonai Echad. Ve'ahavta et Adonai Elohecha, be'chol levavcha, u'vecol nafshecha, u'vechol me'odecha...*" ("Hear, O Israel, the Lord is our God, the Lord is one. And you shall love the Lord your God, with all your heart, with all your soul, with all your might...")

From memory, I wrote an entire paragraph from Deuteronomy 6:4-9. Remember, I was secular to the core. I hated boring, enforced Ta"nach (Jewish Bible) classes, and other than just saying those two words "*Sh'ma Yisreal*," I hardly knew anything about Jewish liturgy and prayers, not even the continuing verses of *Sh'ma Yisrael*...

When I became fully awake and realized what I had just done, I felt intense embarrassment. I feared my father would kill me for destroying the wall behind me. Sharpies don't erase. I was so distraught by that powerful experience that I stayed home from school, faking a sore throat. I just didn't know what to do with myself and how to handle what had happened in the prior twenty-four hours. I moved some things around in my room, and covered the *Sh'ma Yisrael* with a poster of my heroes at the time, Charlie's Angels.

Years later I understood that was my first encounter with a strong power—a power beyond my capability to understand rationally—with unseen guides who have been leading me to where I need to go using puzzling, bewildering visions. That Chasidic figure that came to see me that evening was possibly an appearance of a guiding spirit. *Sh'ma Yisrael* was his way of communicating with me. Those words were embedded within me, becoming my own private utterance at different times throughout my life.

Part Two:
"My God! How Did I Get Here?"[1]

On October 7, 1995, I was sitting in a waiting lounge at Ben Gurion Airport with one carry on bag, and one big suitcase already stored for the next fifteen hours in the baggage compartment of a Boeing 747. I was aware that I was making the bravest decision of a life, and I felt a need to write down my thoughts in my journal. While awaiting my flight to Kennedy Airport, I jotted down these words:

> *Ok, I guess it is starting. I've been really wanting to get away from this banal, predictable path of nearly every Israeli woman in my generation: a thirty-something-year-old woman, settled somewhere in an average neighborhood in the suburbs of Haifa or Tel Aviv, married to a nice husband, with 2.5 children, a dog in the back yard, monthly mortgage bills, a bi-weekly appointment with Nissim the hairdresser, and membership in the nearest country-club. While I am waiting for the plane to take me to the land of my dreams, America, I am aware that I have no idea where the road is taking me beyond the airplane, but I'm not afraid.*

And so it began. I landed at Kennedy Airport on October 8th, facing a chill for which I was not prepared, being from Israel. Stepping outside the airport, waiting on the curb for an old childhood friend to pick me up, I had a very strange experience that lasted for a few moments. I stopped, took a deep breath, closed my eyes, and felt a thirty-year period of longing simply dissipate into the ground. I was finally home. I could not understand that feeling at the time; it only became clear much later, retrospectively, after a few years of actually living in America. But I did know that my life-long desire to "go home" was finally satisfied. Go home? But I've never been here before! (Oh yes, but I have . . .)

Second Vision: I was Once on the East Coast

> *"Summer's here and the time is right for dancin' in the street!"*[2]

Ever since I was a little girl, as my mom still remembers, I used to say: "Ima, when I grow up I am going back home, to America." My mom did not understand how I could want to go "back home to America" when I had never been there before. No one in my family had ever been there and we didn't have any relatives in America. So how could it be? When I was about seven years old the first reel-to-reel recorder was introduced to the twenty-four-years young Israeli nation. My father bought one. It was his indulgence. In the 60s and 70s he would sit for hours listening to the radio and recording songs. All sorts of music from that era—from Europe and America—were playing all the time. Drawn to the music and wishing to be near my father, I used to come and keep him company. He would translate the songs to me the best he could with his limited English. We would sing together and talk about the songs. He would sometimes stand up and show me a dance he and my mother had learned. I remember a song by The Mamas & the Papas, "Dancing in the streets…" I really wanted to be there, with all the happy Americans who were dancing in the streets all across their country. That is one of my first memories of longing to be somewhere else besides war-ridden Israel (it was the era of the Six-Day and Yom Kippur Wars). I began to long for the opportunity to leave one day, but I had no idea how or when it might happen.

And then I had my second vision. I was about sixteen-years-old and was going through puberty coupled with a major rebellious period. I couldn't stand school. I hung out with much older people, started to smoke cigarettes and began wearing "hippie" clothes. One night I went dancing with people whose names I no longer remember. We went to The Tea House in Carmel, a hang-out for the *frikim* ("freaks" in Israel back then was a name for "cool people"). I was dancing and moving ecstatically, breathing in all kinds of scents, smoke, and a variety of *minei besamim*, and all of a sudden I saw it in my mind. I was standing in an open green field covered with yellow and white flowers, raising my arms to the sky. I knew I was somewhere on the East Coast of America. I was staring at a field, I was wearing white and I was happy. The entire vision lasted only a few seconds. I became completely detached from the noise, smoke and other *frikim* around me. The vision made me lose my balance and I nearly fell down, not understanding what had just happened. When I opened my eyes, a line from a song was playing in the background: ". . . somehow I'll find my way home."[3]

I remember coming home later that night, disturbed and shaken to the roots and the core of my soul. My father was at his usual seat, reading his newspaper, listening to the radio by the tape recorder. I sat myself next to him and tried to share what I had just experienced. My father looked at me and said, "Child, I have no idea what you are talking about. It is late, I am tired and frankly you are disturbing my 'me time.'"

That was the end of that conversation—and the end of my father's ability to help me through the deep and complex spiritual path I had embarked upon.

That night also marked my first experience with an unknown component of my life, and I was eager to explore more. I was deeply moved and disturbed after that point, and very restless. I could not find joy in the life that other people my age were leading: school, sports, dating, etc. I dropped out of T'nuat Ha'Noar (a youth movement similar to the American Scouts). I was smoking cigarettes and engaging in philosophical conversations with odd people who crossed my path. I was still hanging out with people twice my age, and locked myself in my room for hours, playing my guitar and singing protest folk songs of the day, both in English and Hebrew. One of my heroes at the time was John Denver. He represented the ol' American boy I was going to marry one day. His songs about West Virginia and the Rocky Mountains continued to fire up my longing to be in America. The Mamas & the Papas were the kind of band I wanted to join.

My twenties are somewhat of a blur. I served in the army's Na"chal, on a kibbutz, and stayed there for a few additional years. While living on the kibbutz, I became a lead singer in two Bluegrass/ Country/Folk bands that performed all across the country (mainly at kibbutzim, folk festivals and barbecue restaurants). In my mid-twenties I moved from being an unhappy "kibbutznik" to being an even unhappier suburbanite, trying to return to city life, this time in Ramat Aviv (N. Tel Aviv). It felt as though I was just floating and moving with a flow that was going nowhere. Though I was busy with the bands, working in record stores to support myself and dating here and there, the main feeling I had was sheer, disturbing nothingness.

Nothing could fill that feeling of emptiness inside of me: no applause from an audience that came to hear our bands; no articles in the paper about the "Israeli Joan Baez"; not even our performances on radio and television shows. I felt so misplaced, so empty, and I could find no peace.

Exploring other Cultures and Spiritual Paths:
My personal "Big Bang"

I tried "spirituality" by joining a Kundelini yoga group in Tel Aviv. That lasted for about two years. My social and spiritual needs were tamed for a while—but then I ended up sleeping with the yoga instructor, and that was the end of that. The loneliness, restlessness and emptiness were increasing by the minute.

And then, a couple of my friends, Suzy and Joe (American-Israelis), told me about a trip they had just taken to the Esalen Institute in Big Sur, California. They said, "...the only thing both of us could think about while participating in the seven-day workshop there was that YOU need to go—you need to be there. You simply have to find a way to get to Esalen! This is the place for you!" They shoved the Esalen Institute catalogue into my hands. I fumbled through the pages. I saw some interesting photos of the place and some intriguing details on a few workshops. I started to get excited about a possible visit—until I saw the prices. How could I ever afford such a trip? How could I afford nearly 1,000 dollars for just one workshop?! Disappointed, I placed the catalogue in the bottom of my desk drawer at the record store and talked myself into forgetting about that place.

Third Vision: Flying Forward in the Chest of an Eagle

Another powerful vision hit my consciousness completely unexpectedly. While living in Ramat Aviv, one of my friends was attending Reedman University, a school for alternative medicine in Tel Aviv. The school was looking for "bodies" to practice on – and of course, I volunteered my body "in the name of science." During the first session with a student of Jin Shin medicine, I was lying on the treatment table, surrendering myself to the gentle touch of the student (I still remember her name—she was also Michal). I started to dose off, and all of a sudden I saw something that nearly made me fall off the table. I saw myself flying with my feet stretched out forward. My head was nestled in a chest of an expressionless Eagle, resting its head on top of mine. We made eye contact and continued flying on forward. The colors around us were deep blue and dark shades of purple. Again, the whole experience lasted only a few, but incredibly powerful, moments.

I heard a soft yet ever-so-present voice from within, in English: "Remember the Eagle, don't forget the Eagle . . ." As I mentioned, the vision was so intense that it startled me awake. My healer asked me what happened, but I was speechless. I had no idea what it was all about and I began to think I was going crazy. I had never seen an eagle before, and certainly not one coupled with a human. And why was the voice making itself heard in English while I was living in Israel? Was I starting to "see things" and "hear voices"? I was seriously scared.

About half a year later, while sitting in a sweat lodge with Chief Red Fox of the Cherokee tribe, a visiting teacher to Esalen at the time, I finally connected the dots. I had a vision of a future that my brain could not yet process.

Crashing

A couple of weeks later I was involved in a very dramatic car crash, the push start of the journey I was about to begin. On my way back to Tel Aviv after visiting my parents' home in Haifa, I lost control of the steering wheel while driving down a steep, hilly road. I immediately started to spin and ended upside-down on a dividing fence between the four lanes of a two-way road. Fortunately, it was nighttime and the traffic around me was sparse. As I was spinning and flipping, something strange was happening: I felt cradled and protected by a yellow, cotton-like light. I know there must have been a terrible screech of wheels, and banging noises—but all I could hear was my own racing heart in an immaculate silence. The whole experience lasted only a few seconds.

While I was lying upside down with my head down and feet up, reality began to kick in. Frantically, I tried to unbuckle myself to get out. I could hear and see people running toward the car, screaming and yelling: "Oh God! Did they get killed? Is there anyone alive in there?" Faces were quickly showing up at the broken windows, the yelling was louder and louder. "Are you okay? Are you injured? Someone! Call an ambulance right away! She's alive! Say *birkat ha'gomel* quickly! *Baruch ha'Shem*, give her a hand . . ."

The people who helped me out marveled at the fact that I could walk, and that I had no apparent injuries. I was shaken, of course, but I only felt two emotions: anger (at myself), and shame for being such a bad driver and for causing such a ruckus, stopping traffic and creating burdening chaos (later on I realized that the dramatic crash was my own personal Big Bang that got me on the road to a new life). That anger and shame somehow allowed my body to shut down and not feel any pain. I had cuts all over my legs and face from the broken window. Some of my wounds were bleeding lightly, and I had to pull a few shards of glass out of different places in my body and face. But I couldn't feel any physical pain.

Someone called my parents, and they quickly came to pick me up. Everyone advised that I should get checked at the hospital, just to make sure there were no internal injuries, but I refused to go. The fact that I was walking around and did not feel any pain was good enough for me. My parents succumbed to my pleas and took me home.

Later on that night, at around 3:00 a.m., I awoke with unbelievable pain in my left leg. My ankle tripled in size, and started to turn blue, black and purple. I thought I was going to die from the pain. I was ready to go to the hospital. My mom drove me there, and I was diagnosed with a broken left ankle and pulled muscles. The doctor put me in a cast and ordered me not to get out of bed for at least two weeks. "Two weeks my ass," I thought. The next day I was already up and about on crutches. I could not be stopped. I wanted to be back in Tel Aviv, running the little record shop, performing with my band and resuming life as if nothing happened. I was still carrying the burden of shame.

The insurance company contacted me a few days later. The agent told me that since the accident was self-inflicted, and that the broken ankle was not considered a "serious injury," I would not get much money from insurance. He advised me that if I wanted to get higher compensation, I should get into the character of a "seriously injured person," which meant never being seen without the crutches, getting a wheel chair if possible, and looking very much in pain when I was out in public. To that I responded: "No way. No monkey business. I will only ask for the amount that is right for such an injury, no more and no less. I am not going to play a role. This needs to be a clean, honest case." (Later on I entertained the idea that my reaction was some kind of an entry test, which I had passed, and which got me to the next level).

A couple of months later, the insurance agent called and asked to meet me, saying, "I have some very good news for you." That happened to be the same day I lost my job at the record store, which was going out of business. The owner was kind enough to add 1,000 shekels to my final paycheck. When I met the agent, he handed me a check that had five digits on it. "This is a miracle," he said. "I have no idea how it happened, but the insurance determined that you should get triple the amount I applied for. This *never* happens. Consider yourself one lucky girl." With two sizable checks in hand, I knew exactly what I was going to do next: plan my trip to Esalen.

Part 3:
I Am Home

I pulled out the catalogue that Suzy and Joe left with me, and started to make some phone calls. I made reservations for a month-long work and study gestalt workshop for December 1st, with a teacher by the name of John Soper. It was 1995 and I did not have access to the Internet or any other communication device apart from my home telephone. I was simply following a voice from within—a force so great that I almost felt as if someone or something was pulling and directing me, very quickly, on to a path that was still unclear. Everything happened so fast, yet was so amazingly organized. I managed to sell all my non-sentimental belongings. I found a nice young student to replace me for my house mate. I found a great bargain on an airline ticket to California with a stopover for a week in Massachusetts and made sure to bring every aspect of my life in Israel to a closure. I said goodbye to my bands with two final concerts, and hosted a party at my house for my closest friends. Suzy and Joe gave me a journal, where I documented everything I was going through, starting on the day of my departure. My journey had begun.

Esalen in Big Sur: Rebirth as I remembered the Eagle!

Following a week in gorgeous Great Barrington, Massachusetts with an old childhood friend, I arrived at the Monterey Airport on October 15, 1995 to start my first workshop at Esalen.

I will never forget my first reaction to that place. I was surrounded by powerful nature: the ocean to the right, magnificent mountains on the left, and Esalen nestled in the center. I remember not being able to say much more than "wow." The beauty of Esalen and Big Sur were beyond anything I had experienced in my life. The natural hot springs, the omnipotence of the ocean, the majesty of the mountains and the spirit of the Esalen Tribe created an environment so powerful that I consider my two-year stay there as a rebirth into a world I was not familiar with at the time: the "interfaith" experience.

Catholicism

I met some very interesting people from different backgrounds, nationalities and religions. My first significant acquaintance was Brother David, who invited me to join him for midnight masses several times at a local hermitage (New Camaldoli Hermitage in the Santa Lucia Mountains). For the first time in my life I got to experience the essence of Christian spirituality. Though I did not accept the wine and bread as the blood and body of Christ, I happily participated in the singing of Gregorian chants that, while I had never heard them before, somehow were familiar enough for me to chant along.

Native Americans and Remembering the Eagle

As mentioned, sweat lodges were periodically held at Esalen. During my first one (where I thought I was going to die from the heat), I had a powerful recollection of the eagle vision of a few months earlier. I understood that I got some sort of a message, a premonition from something that was unknown to me, of a path I was about to embark upon—a path I walked before this lifetime. Esalen was the connecting junction of previous and present experiences, leading to an unforeseen future. Growing up in Israel, other than some "cowboy and Indian" movies starring John Wayne, I had never been exposed to any Native American culture. I felt so moved that I wrote a song called "Remember the Eagle" which I sang while sitting around campfires, telling stories, engaging in artwork or making prayer arrows. It all came so naturally to me; I felt very much at home.

Part 4:
"Becoming Meeka"

There are so many more stories to tell about the amazing Esalen. It was definitely the greatest gift I had received up to that point in my adult life. I equate Esalen to a womb, where I was struggling with old torments, receiving nourishment through a spiritual umbilical cord, and preparing for a future that I did not yet know. But I kept listening to that *bat kol*, that soft inner voice that commanded me "to remember the Eagle"—to follow my heart, my intuition. Esalen was the womb where I spent the first eighteen months in the land of my dreams. Later I was born into a new life, outside of the protective cocoon of the most amazing place on earth.

First Gift: Changing a Name, Becoming "Official"

When my time was up at Esalen in 1997, I moved to Santa Cruz and spent a couple of weeks with some friends, all the while looking for ways to continue my journey. At Esalen I learned of a new concept: "work and study exchange." I worked at Esalen in exchange for room, board and classes, and I heard that other Esalen alumni had moved to the cities and continued to do the same. I found a family at the University of California, Santa Cruz who happened to be looking for a student who would accept room and board in exchange for help with their children. That family was my first introduction into the life I was about to begin. Through them, I learned how to live an urban life in an American city, which meant studying the "laws and ways" of the people who were not from Esalen.

While living with the family and working with the children (and housekeeping), I bought an old Toyota Celica. I still had some funds left from the insurance company in Israel. I applied for a

Social Security Number and for a temporary California driver's license. It was then that I decided to change my name from Michal to Meeka, as I couldn't stand the mistakes people were constantly making. They thought I was a male (Michael), or a Michelle, or pronounced it strangely with the "ch" sound. I invented a new name for myself, one that could not be read nor pronounced any other way than how it is written: Meeka. It was close enough to "Michal," it was original and it was musical. So I became Meeka Levin.

Second Gift: Discovering my Passion for Academia

Soon thereafter I enrolled in a few classes at Cabrillo College in Aptos. Back then—it was pre-9/11—one could apply for a student visa from within the country. I did not have to go back to Israel to become a working student in the States. At Cabrillo College I discovered something about myself that I was not aware of: I was actually in love with academia. In Israel, due to my impatience, restlessness, inner struggles and continuous longing to be somewhere or someone else, I never even finished high school. I had dropped out at the age of sixteen and started to work.

I initially looked at taking classes as a way to stay in the U.S., but once I had the visa, I discovered that I *loved* studying. I busied myself with school activities and received a number of scholarships from organizations that supported women's reentry programs. I was thriving. I discovered my passion for (deep breath) math, music, English literature, anthropology, and other subjects. I familiarized myself with parts of American history I was not aware of, such as the incarceration of Japanese Americans in camps during WWII, a deeper look into slavery, the occupation of Native American lands, and so on. My horizons were expanding so rapidly that I could hardly contain my excitement.

After about six months, the family I was living with left town. Fortunately, I met a woman named Debra in one of my classes. We moved in together and became life-long friends. Debra was a single mother with two young daughters, and they had an extra room in their house. I helped her with the children and housework in exchange for room and board, and continued studying at Cabrillo College.

Jewish Journey Begins (or Resumes)

"Open up our eyes, teach us how to live, fill our heart with joy and all the love You have to give. Gather us in peace, as You lead us to Your name, and we will know that You are One."[4]

Looking for means to support myself, I landed a summer job as a song leader at Camp Tawonga high up in the Sierras. Though my days of spiders, rustic housing, and getting bit by mosquitos ended when I returned my gear to the army at the age of twenty, I decided to go for it. At Tawonga I learned so much about American Jewry. I was introduced to new melodies and became enchanted with the music of Debbie Friedman, Craig Taubman, Jeff Klepper and other Jewish camp songwriters. I participated in Kabbalat Shabbat—North American style—and Shabbat morning Torah sessions. Most of my introduction to North American Judaism began at Camp Tawonga.

In the fall of that year (1998), I was approached by one of my music teachers at Cabrillo who told me that her synagogue, Temple Beth-El (next to the college), was looking for a new junior choir director. Without even asking, she had already set up a meeting for me, saying that she thought I was perfect for the job. I turned white: "I've never conducted a choir before! I am so new to American Judaism!" But I went anyway, and ended up meeting the two people who had a great impact on my Jewish journey: Cantor Paula and Rabbi Rick. Both welcomed me to the congregation, introduced me to a small group of children and said: "Here they are. Teach them Hebrew songs." One of the first songs I taught my group was "Jerusalem of Gold" by Naomi Shemer.[5]

I soon found myself heavily involved with the junior choir, teaching them (and the entire congregation) Chasidic tunes I grew up singing, and Israeli songs I grew up listening to. In return, the congregation invested in my Jewish musical education, sending me to Hava Nashira, where I met those composers I so admired: Craig Taubman, Debbie Friedman (*z"l*), Cantor Jeff Klepper, and the (then young) Rick Recht and Dan Nichols.

At Beth-El, I was also asked to teach Hebrew classes, co-officiate Shabbat services, lead children's High Holidays, and perform a variety of prayer services for adults and children. Before I knew it, I was immersed in Reform Jewish life, soaking in everything I could possibly get my hands on, while strengthening my musical skills in the music department at Cabrillo College. My major became music. I took all the required music classes: theory, solfeggio, world music, music history and so forth. I felt like a thirst-driven sojourner in a desert standing by a fresh water oasis.

To give material expression to my reawakening Jewish spirit, I started to experiment with the wearing of a *kippah*, which felt very strange at first, but eventually became a part of my "preparation for prayer" uniform. Next, I bought my first *talit* (prayer shawl), which was even stranger. In Israel women never wore *talitot* when I was growing up. The exuberance and excitement of rediscovered, reclaimed Judaism also brought up other feelings such as anger, dismay and sadness. Why did I have to leave Israel to discover such a beautiful, all-loving, do's-and-don'ts-free connection with God? Wearing the ever-so-colorful *kippah* and *talit* (with shades of purple and pink on silk) was my own protest against the dark ages' black of Orthodox men and women in Israel. I blamed them for robbing me of the beauty, *kehillah* (community) of other people like myself who love to sing Carlebach, but also Naomi Shemer and Debbie Friedman. I felt frustrated and angry with the Haredim, the Orthodox and ultra-Orthodox streams of Judaism, the only kind of religious Judaism I had known before coming here.

I still struggle with my anger and fear of being ridiculed by Orthodox religious people, but I will discuss that later.

Third Gift: My life partner

> *"Now he [David] was ruddy, and with beautiful eyes, and goodly to look upon. And the Lord said: 'Arise, anoint him; for this is he.' Then Samuel [the prophet] took the horn of oil, and anointed him in the midst of his brethren; and the spirit of the Lord came mightily upon David from that day forward..." 1 Sam. 16:12-13*

In 1998, when I was living with Debra, studying in Cabrillo and working at Temple Beth-El, I met my husband-to-be, Dave Simerly.

Dave, a friend of Debra's, was working for Apple Computer at the time and came to install a new program on her old computer. It was, as they say, love at first sight. We dated for a couple of years and decided to get married. He was a non-Jew, and we had a non-religious ceremony. Dave's background was a non-issue for us when we got married.

Kol D'mama Daka: The Sound of Thin Silence[6]

I continued to work and explore the essence of my Jewish identity. I was engaged in a variety of volunteer activities, like taking my junior choir to sing at local retirement homes and singing for Passover at interfaith *seders* with non-Jewish congregations in the area.

All the while a soft yet consistent voice kept nagging at me from within my soul. It said: "You have to make a deeper commitment. You have the voice. Become a clergy woman. Be a cantor." And, just like at the beginning of my journey when Suzy and Joe told me about Esalen, I could not figure out how I was going to study for such a commitment. A million questions were swarming in my head. So I did what I did best: I stored the idea in one of the deep drawers of my being, and tried to forget about all the crazy cantor nonsense.

Academic Endeavor Continues

When I got married I was also in the process of transferring from Cabrillo to San Jose State University to continue my undergraduate degree in music education. At that time, the idea of a cantorial school started to percolate a little louder in my soul. I remember one significant moment in particular when I was co-leading a Friday service with Rabbi Rick in Santa Cruz. When it ended, a congregant came up to me, took my hands in hers and said: "Your voice brought tears to my eyes. Your singing evoked old memories in me that I had completely forgotten. I really think you should become a cantor." It was then that I asked Rabbi Rick what he thought about this crazy idea. Thinking for a couple of seconds he responded: "Yes, I think that might be where you are headed. What a great moment, you have my blessing..."

I began to explore a variety of possible and impossible options for graduate studies, and finally came across a program in Los Angeles at a school that later became my home for four years: the Academy for Jewish Religion, California (AJRCA). Although I was immersed in Reform Judaism, the movement's Hebrew Union College (HUC) had no cantorial program in the Western States. I felt conflicted. I only wanted to be ordained in the Reform movement—not Conservative, and definitely not Orthodox (which prohibits female cantors anyway). So the AJRCA, a trans-denominational school, felt like a good option. I knew I would have to travel, but at least it was on the West Coast.

I also had a significant and most inspiring conversation with Cantor Jeff Klepper, a Reform cantor, while I was attending my second (and last) Hava Nashira workshop in Oconomowoc, Wisconsin. I found myself walking next to him on the way to dinner. I shared with him the nagging voice within me: my thoughts on becoming a cantor at a trans-denominational school, even though I was Reform to the core of my being. I asked if he thought I could still find work in a Reform congregation in spite of the fact that I would be graduating from a non-HUC school. Jeff looked at me and said, "In my experience, at the end of the day, a congregation will hire you based on who you are, your talent, your experience and personality, not based on the diploma and the school you attended. If you are meant to be a cantor and to work at a Reform congregation, you will find it, and they will find you. Trust the process, trust your own intuition and inner voice."

Cantor Klepper's words gave me the push and encouragement that I needed. Upon completing four years of study at the AJRCA, I found myself on the *bimah* (pulpit) being installed at the congregation that had become my spiritual place: Temple Emanu-El in San Jose, California.

Part 5:
Coming Home

My new home. A place for me to love *Adonai* with all my soul, with all my heart, and all my might.

In August of 2006 I began flying down to Los Angeles each week, staying one to three days and taking courses at the AJRCA for the next four years. A year into my schooling, I was asked to work with a group of adult musicians for an upcoming Shabbat Shira service at Temple Emanu-El in San Jose, where I occasionally subbed for the cantorial soloist. I also led some song sessions with the school children, while continuing to do freelance song leading and teaching classes at a few Jewish schools and congregations in the Bay Area. Working with the adults for Shabbat Shira ended up being a remarkably enjoyable experience for me, and I was asked to continue working with the group for another service.

At that time my husband was about to complete his Jew-by-choice (conversion) process with Temple Emanu-El's young, dynamic and off-the-wall rabbi, Dana Magat. My husband used to *love* studying with Dana, and I found myself warming up to him as well as we co-led a few Shabbat services. And I started to fall in love with the congregation, with the children and the adults I was working with.

Around then the congregation decided it would look to hire a full-fledged cantor for the first time in a very long time (the congregation was established in 1862). Naturally, they turned to HUC. The same quiet yet powerful voice from within started to get louder and louder: "I am loving this place. What if . . ."

Fourth Gift: Becoming Temple Emanu-El's Cantor

My husband encouraged me to think about it. I was so scared because, while I enjoyed being there, deep inside I didn't know if I could yet work as a cantor, so soon into my schooling. This, despite the fact that congregants were coming up to me at the end of services asking, "Why aren't you our cantor? Gosh, I hope that you do apply for the position!" I remember a conversation I had with my husband, as well as one I had with a friend from school. Both said to me, "You are bringing to the table remarkable qualities and qualifications. You come from Israel. You speak Hebrew. You have a vast knowledge of music from both countries. You read

Torah backwards and forwards. You can chant Torah and Haftara trope upside down. You have life experiences and a spiritual drive others can only dream of or read about in books. You have a strong will. Look how far you have come since landing in America with a suitcase in your hand and a guitar on your shoulder. You are a Sabra! You are tough and assertive yet compassionate, and you love people. Go for it!"

Simultaneously encouraged and terrified I wrote a list of the top ten reasons why the temple should hire me as their cantor. I handed the envelope with a shaking hand to Dana, between the *Ma Nishtanah* and the Hillel Sandwich as we led a congregational Passover *seder* in 2006.

Apparently Dana saw the potential in me too, and very excitedly announced to the committee that perhaps the search was over. He recommended me for the position.

That was one of my happiest moments, and I found myself, again, feeling at home. Somehow I found my way home.

And so I began working at Temple Emanu-El as a cantorial intern. I learned hands-on from Dana and the congregants while strengthening my theoretical and cantorial repertoire at AJRCA with some of the finest teachers I have encountered.

One teacher in particular, a Sephardic rabbi named Daniel Bouskila, helped me to close a circle and open a new one. Embracing me as a fellow clergy person and showing appreciation for my talents as a musician, writer and free-thinker, Rabbi Bouskila helped me to see that not all Orthodox men are sexist or chauvinist or lack respect for women in our profession.

Rabbi Bouskila's support helped me to complete the program in four years instead of five, thanks to my Hebrew skills and the fact that I took extra classes normally required for student rabbis. My thesis subject was Naomi Shemer, which later became a chapter in a book, *Emotions in Jewish Music: Personal and Scholarly Reflections*. My colleague Jonathan Friedmann and I collaborated in writing the chapter, as well as working on arrangements for my senior recital.

Part 6:
Challenges

Childless Mother, Bareness

> *"Sing, barren woman, you who never bore a child; burst into song, shout for joy, you who were never in labor; because more are the children of the desolate woman than of her who has a husband," says the Lord. Enlarge the place of your tent; Stretch out the curtains of your dwellings, spare not; Lengthen your cords and strengthen your pegs."*
> - Isaiah 54:1-2

I started writing this essay about a year ago. I knew that when I reached this section it would be quite a challenge. I have lost count of the drafts I have written, scratched out, added to, deleted and rewritten. Writing about not having children has been excruciating for me, in so many different ways.

I realize my journey might be perceived as unusual for a variety of reasons, one of them being that unlike most Jewish families, Dave and I do not have children. Since early childhood, I thought that when I grew up I would marry the man of my dreams and have two children with him. I now see that way of thinking as the result of a collective cultural imprint (a desperate desire to fit in), rather than my own individual connection to the whole, complete picture of my path.

The time I spent at Esalen was like a rebirth—a second chance at a life I created for myself. But it happened fairly late in my physical years. I was thirty when I came to America, and it would take more than a decade before Dave and I became a family. By the time we got married, I only started my journey as a cantor, and it became challenging to do it all in "one breath." I was going to school (making up for lost years of education), working many hours at my job, and working on creating and maintaining a home with my life partner.

A well known Talmudic idiom says, *"Tafasta merubeh lo tafasta, tafasta muat tafasta."* (If you have seized a lot, you have not seized; if you have seized a little, you have seized.) This phrase really captured my feelings: how could I possibly do everything well at the same time and succeed, rather than feel like a failure again?

During the first few years of our marriage, when I still had a chance of fertility, we tried to get pregnant. I went to Western fertility specialists and visited an acupuncturist twice a week. The conventional medicine OB/GYN gave me hormone pills, while the acupuncturist provided me with bitter Chinese herbs. I read many books about infertility, and became very moody. I felt heartbroken every month as my body cried with disappointment, shedding tears of blood out of my empty womb.

My family in Israel was not particularly helpful. Their general thought was that I wasn't trying hard enough. Some family members uttered some pretty nasty things, like "What, you are not a woman?" and "You'd rather spend money on school than on pregnancy." I was scared, confused, restless and frustrated. Something that I thought I wanted very much simply was not happening for me. Following an ultrasound during one of my last visits, the doctor delivered the bad news: my eggs were "too old." I wouldn't be able to conceive the natural way. I had to consider in vitro fertilization, surrogacy or adoption. I was devastated.

Then, one day, while walking along a nature trail in our area, I spotted a woman coming toward me with a baby stroller, accompanied by a large, magnificent dog. I felt sheer excitement. I approached the woman, with my full attention—on the dog. I became aware of something significant shifting within me. I was 40 years old, and I finally opened up to the idea of not having children. The grief and anxiety started to lessen and I was becoming comfortable with the idea of concentrating on my schooling, my religious calling, and all the possible goodness Dave and I could share together as a couple.

Over the years we adopted three magnificent schnauzers into our lives (Simba, Schnitzel and Dahlia). They became a part of our late-blooming family.

Today

My main struggle is with questions and comments I am either asked directly, or detect on the faces of other Jewish clergy and congregants. I am often asked, "Aren't you scared you'll regret not having children?" When I visit in Israel I am not asked if I have children, but rather how many children I have. It feels as though everyone has accepted the idea that a Jewish family must have children. I find that most Jews automatically assume that since I am happily married, serve as a clergy person, and love children so much, I must have children of my own.

I know that being Jewish, married and not having children is a rare combination. Truth being told, now and then I do experience a pain of loss. At times, I feel something similar to a need to apologize. I also feel judged, especially by other members of the clergy. I feel looked down upon, as if I am robbing Jewish heritage of its future by not raising the future Jewish generation.

The ideal of raising children is ingrained deep in my soul, which is connected to thousands of years of Jewish consciousness and identity. Even though I know better—and mostly feel complete and at peace with my life as is—not being a parent makes me feel somewhat separated from the rest of the tribe.

I haven't found much written in Jewish liturgy about childless Jewish couples and homes. It feels like there is some sort of "don't ask, don't tell" mentality in the collective Jewish mindset. I did find, however, one excerpt in a book I read many years ago that gave me some solace:

> *Having children is not the only purpose of marriage. Not every Jewish couple is prepared to go through medical procedures that can be costly and unpleasant. Not every infertile couple chooses to go through the emotional trauma of adoption. Judaism does consider it improper for a fertile couple to be childless. Yet Jewish couples who are infertile should not feel that they have nothing to live for. Judaism sees the essential purpose of marriage as companionship. It teaches that even people who are unable to have children should be married and establish a household.[7]*

I also know deep in my soul that being a mother does not necessarily mean having my own children. I care for and teach children of all ages, almost every day of my life. Then I get to go home to the warm, sacred nest Dave and I have built for ourselves, knowing that I will always care for others with great motherly energy, without having to go through *"beetzev teldi"*—the pain of giving physical birth.

Loneliness of an Eagle Woman

> *Leaders are like eagles. They don't flock, you find them one at a time.*
> - Anonymous

> *...but they who wait for the Lord shall renew their strength; they shall mount up with wings like eagles; they shall run and not be weary; they shall walk and not faint.*
> - Isaiah 40:29-31

> *Who satisfies you with good so that your youth is renewed like the eagle's.*
> - Psalm 103:5

I do get lonely sometimes. With my Israeli family so far away, I haven't even met my now two-year-old niece, the youngest addition to my sister's family. Due to my hectic schedule, it is hard to foster friendships when my days off seldom match those of other people. So I spend a lot of time alone. My love for nature compels me to take the dogs to the beach or for hikes in the woods.

Having children or not, the feeling of being separated, isolated and lonely in the scary desert called "life" was imprinted in the Jewish soul in the days of old, when the Torah was written and the Jewish people were becoming a nation. Each of us experiences loneliness in a different way, as we walk on separate paths.

I was born a Levite, a woman of the tribe of priests. I was led to a life of servitude through visions, while presented with incredible opportunities. I don't know "what" or "who" God is, but I experience many moments of "godliness" in my everyday life. I am driven to continue serving any way I can (recently I have been a Jewish chaplain for our local jails), and I continue to look for ways to strengthen my connection with God through service to others.

Part 7:
Te'filat Ha'lev, the Prayer of My Heart

Adonai seftai tiftach u'fi yagid tehilatecha—O, Eternal God open my lips, that my mouth may declare Your Glory.

It is 2012. I am standing on a podium, looking at hundreds of cheering people from all walks of life. With me stand the mayor of San Jose, city council members, political dignitaries and veterans, some of whom are wearing military uniforms and colorful symbols. For the third consecutive year I was invited to be the chaplain and deliver the invocation for this ceremony, which coincides with Santa Clara's Veterans Day Parade. I briefly look at myself from a distance, and I can't help but ask, "My God, how did I get here?" I feel so proud and honored to be of service to the country that gave me a second chance at having a fulfilling life.

Coincidentally, about a year ago I read an interesting article in the Israeli newspaper *Yediot Achronot* about female pilots who completed an intense course in the Israeli Air Force.[8] The opening sentence made me chuckle: "Since the Israeli Air Force was established, this would have sounded like a joke: when Ezer Weizman[9] heard of the lawsuit of Alice Miller, sixteen-years-ago, he asked her if she's ever seen a man knitting socks..." In 1995, the Supreme Court of Israel heard a petition from a twenty-three-year-old South African immigrant to Israel, Alice Miller, a woman who wanted to be tested for acceptance to the IAF Flight School. Alice won her case that November and her petition led to the opening of the school to women and a long process that would pave the way for females to serve in combat positions in the IAF. Although she succeeded in opening the doors of the flight school to women, Alice herself never crossed the threshold, having failed the medical examinations. But Miller won the case, and women became eligible to receive the *semel ha'knafayim* (Israeli Air Force wings badge). They became a part of something that is no longer seen as weird: Israeli women combat pilots.

Women around the world are on their way to exploring more and more roles that, up until the last thirty or forty years, were considered reserved for men only. These include air force combat pilots and other military personnel, high power executives in the business world, and female clergy members, which we see more and more of today. As an Israeli, I've seen women like Golda Meir and Ge'ula Kohen lead political parties well before other women around the world were able to do so. But it is only now that I am starting to see and read about women in Israel becoming part of fields that, during my childhood, were never possible, like female pilots and clergy. I'd like to believe that in the near future, these phenomena will not be so interesting.

Where to From Here?

I am the Eagle, I live in high country in rocky cathedrals that reach to the sky.[10]

The female pilots spread their wings and are now flying airplanes. I spread a different set of wings. In 1995 I got on a plane that brought me to the United States to begin a journey that eventually enabled me to serve as a clergy woman: a spiritual leader of a congregation in San Jose. Outside of my congregational work, I do community service as a chaplain, officiating at Memorial Day services in our area and visiting Jewish inmates at our county jail. I feel I am in a period of incubation, collecting details and information on a path I'd like to continue to pursue.

This is the private prayer of my heart: For as long as I am able I will continue to spread my wings and fly like a proud eagle, soar as high as I am capable, and trust that, if it is meant to be, I shall humbly continue to serve humanity and experience holy moments in the greatest cathedral of all: God's universe. *Ken Yehi Ratson—* May this be God's will.

NOTES

1. Talking Heads, "Once In A Lifetime," *Remain in the Light*, 1991, Sire, compact disc.

2. Martha & The Vandellas, "Dancin' in the Street," *Dance Party*, 1964, Gordy, vinyl.

3. Jon and Vangelis, "I'll Find My Way Home," *The Friends of Mr Cairo*, 1981, Polydor, vinyl.

4. Jeff Klepper, "Open Up Our Eyes," in *The Complete Shireinu*, ed. Joel N. Eglash (New York: Transcontinental, 2001), 263.

5. Many years later Naomi Shemer became the subject of my thesis, and "Jerusalem of Gold" was a major song at my senior recital for cantorial ordination at the Academy for Jewish Religion, California. The thesis was condensed into a book chapter, "Naomi Shemer's Artistic Expression: Poetry, Prayer, or Both?" in *Emotions in Jewish Music: Personal and Scholarly Reflections*, ed. Jonathan L. Friedmann (Lanham, MD: University Press of America, 2012), 5-29.

6. From I Kings 19:12. This is one of my favorite biblical phrases. It is so short, yet so powerful, especially in the Hebrew language. "Kol" is a voice (also mentioned in Exodus 19:19). "Dak" means thin (also mentioned in Isaiah 29:5). "Damam" is silence or stillness (mentioned in Exodus 15:16). The verse in I Kings relates to Elijah's powerful experience with God.

7. Michael Gold, *And Hannah Wept: Infertility, Adoption, and the Jewish Couple* (Philadelphia: Jewish Publication Society, 1988), 53.

8. Yossi Yehoshua, "Porsot Kanaf" ["Spreading their Wings"], *Yediot Achronot* 23 Dec. 2011.

9. Ezer Weizman was the seventh President of Israel, first elected in 1993 and re-elected in 1998. Before his presidency, Weizman was commander of the Israeli Air Force and Minister of Defense.

10. John Denver, "The Eagle and the Hawk," *Aerie*, 1971, RCA, vinyl.

Cantor Miriam Eskenasy brings her gifts and knowledge as an ordained Cantor, musician, and teacher to the Jewish community. Born in Bucharest, Romania, to Zionist parents, Miriam immigrated to Israel when she was ten years old. It was there that she discovered her talent for languages, becoming fluent in Hebrew, French and English in addition to her native Romanian.

At sixteen, she and her family came to the United States. Miriam graduated from Queens College of C.U.N.Y. For the next twenty years, Miriam lived, worked, married and raised a family in New York City.

Miriam continued singing and performing opera and eventually joined the Rottenberg Chorale, a Jewish choir in New York. During her ten-year involvement with the chorale, Miriam realized that singing Jewish music strengthened her own identity and passion leading her to choose it as her life's work. In 1998, she was accepted at the Hebrew Union College-Jewish Institute of Religion (HUC-JIR) in New York and studied Jewish music, as well as Jewish history, philosophy, liturgy, Torah, biblical grammar and more. In 2002 Miriam was ordained as a Cantor. Her Master's thesis focused on the music of the Sephardi community in Romania during the nineteenth and twentieth centuries.

After serving congregations on the East Coast, Cantor Miriam came to Chicago where she currently resides, to become the Cantor of KAM Isaiah Israel Congregation in 2008.

6
THE SLOW ROAD TO THE CANTORATE
Miriam Eskenasy

Romania

I WAS BORN IN BUCHAREST, ROMANIA IN 1950. Romania was very much communist then, and even though I knew as a child that I was Jewish, that was *all* I knew about my Jewishness. My mother would travel outside of Bucharest every year to some secret source to buy a box of matzah for Passover—not because we celebrated the holiday, but rather to show me what Jews ate on Passover. My parents also always fasted on Yom Kippur, but that was the extent of their Jewish observance.

Other than that, my Jewish experiences in Romania were very limited. There was one other Jewish kid in my class and our parents, together with most of Bucharest's Jewish population who dared, applied to immigrate to Israel. In anticipation of this great event, our parents sent us both to *cheder*, a school where Jewish education took place. This was a very mysterious affair at my seven years of age. Sometimes we went up a very old shaky staircase to the teacher's attic where we learned the *alef beit* and basic Hebrew reading (I have faint memories of the experience). After one year, my classmate's family received papers to go to Israel and I refused to go to *cheder* by myself. So my formal Jewish education ended.

I did have other Jewish experiences in communist Romania. One was of going to synagogue with my next-door neighbor, Mr. Abramowitz. Mr. Abramowitz was not afraid of the communists because he was older and he did not care. It was Simchat Torah and I was very little. I was surrounded by many men and it was very noisy and crowded. I can still remember the shape of Mr. Abramowitz's hand, which I was holding tightly.

Another time, a Yiddish theater group came to Bucharest and we saw a production of *The Diary of Anne Frank* in Yiddish, which neither me nor my mother spoke. Also, the earphones that were supposed to give us a simultaneous translation were broken. So, although very aware that we were doing something exciting and dangerous at the same time, I did not get much out of the play. Incidentally, Yiddish theater was invented in Romania and one of its early stars, Molly Picon, came to the United States where she had a successful movie career.

Jewish experiences that actually strengthened my Jewish identity were not numerous but they were very important. Many of my classmates used to call me derogatory names like "Jidanca," which is really how I knew that I was Jewish! One of them actually got punished when I told the teacher (I felt vindicated) and another was chased and beaten by another classmate who was not Jewish, but who was incensed at the calling of names.

Although I did not realize it then, as our own departure from Romania was nearing many of my parents' friends and relatives were already leaving for Israel. Most of them did not live in Bucharest (my parents are from a city named Craiova), but came to Bucharest to board the train that would take them to Vienna, or some other destination in the West and from there to Israel. Most of these friends and family would naturally stay at our house before they left.

This is how I found out that my parents were ardent Zionists: The night before someone left, my parents would offer a nice meal after which all the windows would be closed and the curtains drawn. All the guests would stand up and sing *Hatikvah*—not too loud because the communists had ears everywhere—the official song of the Zionist Congress and now the national anthem of Israel. To me, just a small child then, this was electric. Everyone was filled with a hope and a yearning and the knowledge that better days were ahead (the meaning of *Hatikvah*). And, even though I did not understand much, I was swept along and had a love of this unknown exotic place before I even set foot on the shores of Haifa in 1961.

So I knew I was Jewish, I knew the Hebrew alphabet, and I had a yearning for Israel. All a good start.

In March 1961 we were on a train from Bucharest to Hungary and then to Vienna. A bus from Vienna took us to Venice where we spent three magical days. The most exciting moment, which made a very lasting impression on me, was a visit to the ghetto. We did not speak Italian, and the Italian Jews behind the gate did not speak Romanian, although the two languages are very close. How did we communicate? The lady behind the gate revealed a *Magen David* (Jewish Star) hung around her neck, pointed to it and gave us a questioning look. For the first time in my life I saw Jews openly admitting their Jewishness. We all nodded "yes" with tears in our eyes! The climax of the day came with a visit to the synagogue, which was very stately with elegant red velvet and dark mahogany everywhere, and the sun glistening through the high windows into the dark sanctuary. I was speechless with awe. We were free to be who we were and no one was going to throw us in jail because of it.

Israel

Shikun—Givat Olga—army base to the left—Mediterranean in front—village to the right—neighbors from other countries—sixth grade—learning Hebrew—making new friends—*Kibbutz Galuyot* (ingathering of the Diaspora)—the acclimatization Ben Gurion dreamed about and achieved. In three short months I became Israeli and never looked back. We were Zionists and Zionism was our religion.

But living in Israel automatically meant more exposure to religion, traditions and observance because, in 1961, Shabbat was observed everywhere in Israel, not just in Jerusalem. On Friday afternoons my neighbors from Morocco (or maybe it was Tunisia) would go to the market to buy chickens, dress in white long robes, and celebrate Shabbat. My neighbors from some *shtetl* in Romania would *kasher* their dishes before Passover outside in a sand pit, and others from other countries would go to the synagogue. We did not do any of these things. My first "*seder*" consisted of eating matzah-ball chicken soup in the kitchen while listening to a sweet boy's voice singing the four questions on the radio. As a student at Hebrew Union College (HUC) years later I learned that ninety-six percent of Israelis, even the most secular such as us, celebrate Passover in some form. Matzah-ball soup at the kitchen table with the radio is how my family celebrated.

As a teenager, I also observed Yom Kippur. I used to walk with my friends, who were also immigrants from Romania, passing by the synagogue and looking through the window to see Yizchak Rabin and Moshe Dayan inside. We did not dare enter. We would not have known what to do.

Life in Israel was very hard for my parents (not for me), and after five-and-a-half years they became cured of their Zionism and looked to leave the beautiful magical land that had given me a sense of identity like no other place ever had. Before we left, I decided I would join an army singing group when the time came for me to serve (Lehakat ha Nachal was my favorite group). To give myself the best chance, I enrolled in a music conservatory on Rehov Lilenblum in Tel Aviv where I studied theory, piano and voice. But alas, after a couple of months I was on a ship to New York!

Columbus, Ohio

I graduated from Eastmoor High School in Columbus, Ohio in 1968. I never questioned my parents' decisions up to that point, but to take a sixteen-year-old out of an environment in which she thrived and bring her to a completely foreign and unfamiliar place was sheer cruelty. It is a miracle I survived. Much of my survival is owed to the Jewish community in Columbus.

My Jewish classmates at Eastmoor were very supportive and helpful, although we are probably better friends now with the advent of Facebook than we were back then. The kindest act I remember in my first few weeks came from a schoolmate named Amy Stern, who brought me a pair of gym socks and gave me fifteen cents to buy *The Chariot*, the school paper that ran an article about me. But my best friend and main supporter was Mr. Griffin, my music teacher. Every morning he would come in at 7:00 a.m. to teach me privately. He coached me on the solo from Handel's *Messiah*, "O Thou that Tellest Good Tidings to Zion," which I sang at a school competition with the choir. He taught me principles of theory not covered in class so I could pass the entrance exam for the music program at Ohio State University (OSU). He worked with me on my very first classical song, "Caro Mio Ben," for my OSU audition. He was also the bassoonist in the Columbus Symphony, and he would pick me up, together with a few classmates, and bring us to concerts for some real music appreciation. In short, the last two years of high school were a musical awakening for me, which whetted my appetite and gave me a sense of purpose and direction. Whether it was to be the star of an Israeli army group or on the stage of an opera house, it was music and I loved it all.

Parallel with my general music education, I received Jewish musical exposure at the local Conservative synagogue, Tifereth Israel. My mother and I were welcomed with open arms and supported by the Columbus Jewish community in the best traditional sense. We had tickets to High Holidays (our first ever). I had a job in the Sunday school teaching music to little children—a job I loved. Most importantly, I was drafted into the choir. There, for the first time, I was exposed to the music of Louis Lewandowski and other classical Reform composers whose music was sung during the High Holidays. I remember our choir director, Rabbi Saul Wachs, lovingly guiding us. I remember *Habein Yakir Li*, a Lewandowski composition that was so beautiful it made me cry. Although very young—still a teenager—and very new to it all, Rabbi Wachs gave me a couple of solos. I fell completely in love with synagogue music.

One has to understand that the thought of becoming a cantor never entered my mind in those days. It was 1967-1968, and I had never seen a woman on the *bimah*. It would be at least seven years before women cantors would be accepted in the Reform movement, and much longer in the Conservative movement. So, while I loved singing in the choir of Tifereth Israel, I continued to pursue my classical music studies.

I became a music major at OSU. My education laid a foundation I found very useful years later as I entered cantorial school at the HUC, and has served me well throughout my career—even though I was only a music major for two years. That was a time of my awakening independence and pursuit of my dream of becoming a singer, which then meant being an opera singer. I was living in the French House at Ohio State and was involved in French culture and activities, along with studying classical music, theory, sight-singing (still tough for me) and composition. I continued my involvement with the synagogue and also found time to work for the Hebrew professor at OSU, Yaakov Mashiach. I maintained a very strong sense of Israeli identity (I still do) and a part of me felt compelled to keep some involvement with the Jewish community.

While at OSU, my parents had moved to New York and demanded that I join them there. There came a point in my life that for the first time I wanted to disobey them. I felt it was right for me to remain at OSU even if it meant that I had to work to support myself and go to school part time. Ultimately, I did not have the courage or the American upbringing to take such a drastic step. I left OSU and the music, and went to New York.

New York

The Aaron Copland School of Music at Queens College was in its infancy in 1970. Queens College was known as the school that Simon and Garfunkel were thrown out of (maybe it was just Simon), and the school of Carole King and Marvin Hamlish. There was no performance major in 1970 and I lost over thirty credits and a year's work in the transfer. My parents were pushing very hard for me to study something "sensible" instead. Under pressure from them, and disappointed with the music department, I earned my bachelor's in French literature instead, which again did not mean that I stopped singing or being Jewish. My continuing Jewish education at Queens included a class in French Jewish Literature (very eye-opening) with Professor Rabbi Sungolowski, where we studied works like Albert Memi's *La Statue de Sel* and Roger Ikor's *Les Eaux Meles*, and an introductory class in Jewish music with Professor Arbie Orenstein, in which I was introduced to cantillation and other fundamentals. Finally, upon graduating in 1973, I joined the Queens College Opera Workshop under its director, composer Hugo Weisgall. I stayed in the opera workshop until my daughter was born in 1979.

Weisgall was a well-known Jewish composer and was at that time head of the cantorial school at the Jewish Theological Seminary (JTS). So, although not officially, my Jewish musical education continued. I attended all the cantorial recitals at JTS, which I loved, learned about famous Jewish artists such as Gertrude Stein (we sang *The Mother of Us All*, an interesting opera with a libretto by Stein and music by Virgil Thomson), and Ezra Lederman, in whose opera, *The Hunting of the Snark*, I starred. Finally, as a culmination of that era, I starred as Leah in *The Dybbuk*, an opera based on the Yiddish story by S. Ansky and composed by the head of the music department of Queen's College, Joel Mandelbaum.

At the time I was doing all of this I was not thinking about my Jewishness. I had very few Israeli friends, I did not attend synagogue, and I was very serious about singing opera, performing various roles big and small with the Bel Canto Opera Company, Amato Opera, Stuyvesant Opera, and other small companies in New York City. For a few years, I had lost touch with my Jewish side. With the birth of my children, it became increasingly important for me to practice Judaism and pass the little I knew about it on to them.

Off went my oldest daughter Carin, at the age of four, to an Orthodox yeshiva. For most Israelis in the 1970s, Orthodox Judaism (and to a lesser extent Conservative Judaism) was the only Jewish variety we knew anything about. I had heard of Reform, but dismissed it as watered-down Judaism—almost resembling a different religion. After one year at the yeshiva, it became clear that Orthodox Judaism was not for us. P.S. 69 awaited us with open arms and both of my daughters had wonderful experiences there and at other wonderful public schools in New York City. They eventually graduated from LaGuardia High School and are now both professional musicians.

Being Jewish, which was so easy in Israel, became a big project in New York, especially when looking for the right balance in the Jewish education of my daughters. I turned to the synagogue religious school. My local Conservative synagogue, the Jewish Center of Jackson Heights, had about five children in the whole program of varying ages, and my daughters attended the Hebrew school there for about three years. A new rabbi, who insisted that my children attend junior congregation on Saturdays once a month, put an end to their Jewish religious education. We already had a religion and it was called *music*. Each Saturday from 8:00 a.m. until 4:00 p.m., my daughters attended the Queens College Center for Preparatory Studies in Music. Even the Hebrew School teacher advised me against choosing the synagogue over the music program and, as such decisions are always hard, I made the difficult choice to pull them out of religious school. Really, they were kicked out by an insensitive rabbi for not coming to a half-hour service once a month. Doing this felt right to me, as I did not feel comfortable with being dictated how much Judaism I should practice or teach my daughters.

The perfect solution was ETGAR, a Hebrew after school program for children of Israeli parents. It was Judaism as I had experienced it in Israel and it felt comfortable to me. It consisted mainly of modern Hebrew language instruction and holiday celebrations.

My personal needs, though, took me back to the Jewish Center of Jackson Heights where I once again became involved with singing in the choir and attending services on Friday nights. The rabbi at that time (a new rabbi) had just come from Israel, and he was a cantor/rabbi with a beautiful *basso profundo* voice. Meeting him and working with him for the few years he was there was instrumental in my later decision to apply to the HUC. He wanted to coach me in *chazzanut* (cantorial art) and believed firmly in my abilities. But I was hesitant for several reasons:

• Coming from a non-observant family, I did not feel qualified to represent God and the Jewish religion to others, to stand on the *bimah*. I felt it would be inauthentic.

• I did not want to do things halfway. Private coaching was okay, but I felt that if I wanted to become a cantor, I should follow proper procedures and go through a formal program of study.

• At the time I had two small children and was helping my husband with his architectural business, and becoming a cantor would have required major changes in family dynamics I was not ready for.

• I did not feel that women could be up on a *bimah*. To me, even in the eighties, it seemed wrong.

So I did not apply right away. The cantor/rabbi of the Jewish Center of Jackson Heights went back to Israel and a new rabbi came. I finally did apply in 1988, together with a friend from my Queens College days who sang with me in the synagogue choir, Cantor Judy Neimark. We were both invited to apply formally by Cantor Goldstein, then head of HUC's School of Sacred Music. The application filled me with dread and I did not think I could manage it, especially since the first year of studies was in Israel. What would I do with the children? How would I fund this venture? What would happen to my marriage? When I told my husband about this idea he laughed, which put a damper on the entire project. I found out that I could commute to Philadelphia once a week to study there for my first year instead of going to Israel. But even that proved to be too difficult to manage with a budding architectural business and two children. So my friend, Judy, went on and entered the cantorial program at HUC, and I kept searching.

It was not until ten years later that I finally applied again. By then I was divorced. My oldest daughter was a bassoon major at Juilliard and my youngest daughter was in high school. I had an unhappy administrative job and the timing felt right. Once I made up my mind, I never looked back.

One day I took off from work, sang for Cantor Goldstein again, and received an application package from Sara Lee Avery, who told me there would not be enough time to complete everything (two weeks). She advised me to apply the following year. That was all I needed to hear. That afternoon I came home and organized all the paperwork and made a time-line of the entire project. It was a lot of work: calling for transcripts; calling for letters of recommendations; sending out forms; arranging for GRE classes; writing an essay; making doctors' appointments (HUC wanted to make sure applicants were not crazy); and deciding repertoire for the main audition. All the excuses I had given myself ten years before seemed to have disappeared or worked themselves out. I felt I had a calling. All of my life's experiences up to that point had prepared me to be a candidate for the cantorate, and I was finally free to pursue my life's dream: singing Jewish music. I had no idea then how much more I was going to get.

Hebrew Union College

Studying at the Hebrew Union College–Jewish Institute of Religion was a four-year love affair. It was the highlight of my life up to that point, and the love I received from classmates and teachers was almost overwhelming. That does not mean that the program was easy for me. On the contrary.

My fifteen-year-old daughter and I arrived in Israel in September 1998. I did not need to study at the *ulpan* (Hebrew immersion summer program) since, despite not speaking Hebrew for some thirty years, I placed in the highest level Hebrew class. The extra summer months worked in my favor, as I was able to fulfill my obligations in New York and plan the trip of nine months for my younger daughter and myself.

I cannot describe the emotions I felt when we arrived in Israel (it happens every time). My daughter had never been there and I had never lived in Jerusalem. At HUC in Jerusalem I found a community of sixty-two rabbinical, cantorial and education students studying together at our beautiful campus. I could not believe I actually made it happen.

As a French major in college, we studied the philosophy of *la condition humaine* (the human condition), and how we climb the mountain every day and fall right back down every night—how we can never escape that condition. I read in newspapers today about discrepancies in the education of the rich and poor: how few poor people are able to escape their human condition and actually get a decent education and enter into a different socio-economic class. At HUC I was in such a different world. I felt like one of those few privileged kids who got a chance.

What I loved about it the most was the fact that they did not force religion on anyone. They took each of us from our different backgrounds. There was me, a forty-eight-year-old American-Israeli Zionist. There was a Jew-by choice. There was a Reform camp-song leader, a young lady who was searching and searching, a Yiddish-Russian chanteuse, and others. The professors simply instructed us in the basics of Judaism in an objective manner. In the first year they taught us modern Hebrew, literature, Hebrew

Bible, biblical Hebrew grammar, liturgy, the history of Israel, Jewish music history, sight singing, cantillation, weekday *nusach*, synagogue modes, Reform repertoire and other essentials we would need to practice our new craft. Before there were cantorial schools, cantors learned their profession from long apprenticeships to other cantors—a lifetime of knowledge that HUC tried to squeeze into four years of study (now five).

I remember in Paul Liptz's course on Israel's history learning about the different immigration waves to Israel. When he talked about the second wave of immigration, which happened in the late 1950s early 60s, I stood up and announced to the entire class that they were looking at the second wave of immigration, much to everyone's laughter. We formed little communities. I would meet with my classmates Mari and Lori at Café Hess every week for Hebrew conversation (led by me) and in return they would help me with my biblical grammar class. We always studied in *chevruta* (partnership). We had Shabbat dinners together and sang together. When a bomb exploded at *Machane Yehuda* (the open-air market in Jerusalem), we all activated the phone tree and sat glued to the television together for hours. It was an unforgettable year both for me and my daughter. She was in the EIE program, a semester of study abroad sponsored by the Union for Reform Judaism—except that she did it for two semesters instead of one.

I remember her surprise and disgust to read about the battles of Joshua where thousands of women and children were killed for no reason. I remember my rabbinical classmates trying to explain it all to her and help her with her Judaica homework (I sure could not). She studied Hebrew in the *ulpan* and marveled at all the Italian and French Jewish kids in her class. It was an incredible experience for her. The experience was also incredible for me on many levels:

• First, I was in my beloved Israel. I immediately re-adopted my Israeli habit of thirty years before: *chutzpah*. I remember the lady on the Egged (the Israeli bus company) refusing to talk to me until I said *b'vakashah* (please) and *todah* (thank you) and *shalom*. Israel had changed. I traveled north and south with my daughter, I had a reunion with all my

childhood friends in Zahala, and I felt at home everywhere
(except in East Jerusalem).

• Second, I was in school again after twenty-five years. I was
learning many new things, some of which I loved and some I
did not love so much. I did not love cantillation, for instance.
It was something mysterious to me and I did not think I was
supposed to do it. In my Conservative *shul* only men chanted
Torah, and there was a *baal koreh* (a Torah reader). Not even the
hazzan chanted. I had not done my homework about the Reform
movement. I was shocked to learn that I had to chant Torah. I
was ready to go back to New York, and for the first semester I
sat in the class without once volunteering to chant. Of course,
Eli Schleifer, our teacher, did not push me. Rather, he gave me
the lowest passing grade possible (75 percent). Not only did I
improve in the second semester, but I have learned to love the
skill, which I teach with great gusto to our *b'nei mitzvah* in my
very Reform synagogue, where, until a few years ago, only a few
children chose to chant. I have created a chanting frenzy where
even the most unmusical children insist on chanting the Torah.
This is my "claim to fame" as a cantor, and I am hoping it will
continue to be my "bread and butter" as I plan my retirement.

• Third, for the first time in my life I belonged to a community.
I was an urban kid. Sure I had many friends both in Romania
and especially in Israel, but we were not a community such
as my class was that year in Israel. I felt accepted and loved. I
still communicate with many of my classmates, both rabbinic
and cantorial, and even though we no longer have Shabbat
dinners together, I feel fortunate that we crossed paths
and can count on each other forever. (Facebook is a great
facilitator for keeping in touch.)

The magic of Israel, however, did not last forever. We
completed our program in New York and I was assigned my first
student pulpit. Although the sense of community was shattered
in New York with everyone being so spread out, and we were no
longer in my beloved Israel, the enthusiasm continued as I learned
about Judaism and Jewish music in depth. Philosophy with Gene
Borowitz; liturgy with Larry Hoffman; history with Carol Bailin;

traditional *chazzanut* with Jack Mendelson and Izzy Goldstein; Reform repertoire with Benjie Ellen Schiller; coaching with Faith Steinsnyder and Noah Schall. These are all giants in their fields— consummate teachers whose notes, even after eleven years on the pulpit, I still use in my own teachings.

My thesis focused on the music of the Sephardi community of Romania from 1800 to 1941, when the Sephardi synagogue in Bucharest, *Cahal Grande*, was destroyed. Researching material for my thesis was a fascinating process that took me to many different places, from the New York Public Library to Bucharest's Academy of Letters (where archives are kept). I never wanted to stop. At the same time, I felt I had an obligation to myself and my family to finish the paper and actually work as a cantor to gain additional in-depth experience.

When I graduated, I had an academic opportunity at HUC in Jerusalem, but felt compelled to serve a congregation rather than being an academic. Ultimately I could not leave my family and live on a different continent, in a country that was besieged by *piguim* (terrorist bombings). Although I am still a Zionist, I cannot envision a time soon when I would ever return to Zion (other than visit periodically). How could I teach others *chazzanut* without ever serving a congregation? I thought . . .

While a student in New York, I served as the student cantor of East End Temple, which was then located at 23rd and 1st Avenue. To this day, that position remains the best one I ever had. I honed my craft there and made many lifelong connections with congregants. For my first High Holidays I was happy to have a quartet whose members sang in the Metropolitan Opera Chorus. I thought being the cantor was the greatest. I got to sing every Shabbat, my congregants adored me, I worked with great people, and I could earn money to live.

It was not until I graduated that the rose-colored glasses came off. HUC taught us to be idealistic, to seek spirituality. They told us we were equal clergy partners with the rabbis and, generally, they were at least twenty to thirty years behind what was actually happening in congregations across the country. Whereas I was told that my age and experience were pluses in my employability (and for the most part they were—I had several job offers upon graduation), one rabbi questioned me about how long a woman's voice lasted. No one advised me regarding what a good job would be for a fifty-two-year-old-Zionist-Israeli-New Yorker who was also a cantor, but my colleagues and rabbis all had opinions. It was very difficult to make a decision. I eventually chose a young congregation in Westchester instead of an old congregation with a rich musical history in Long Island. What can I say? This choice alone led me on a very different path than I expected.

I anticipated choosing one congregation and staying there until I retired ten or fifteen years down the road. Instead, since 2002, the year of my graduation, I have served four congregations. There are many reasons why I served these different congregations. Some of them were the wrong choices because my criterion was wrong: I based my decision on a synagogue's location or hearsay or, in some cases, because it was the only offer I had. But this was also a difficult period in my personal life. During the past eleven years, I have gone through menopause, severe hearing loss, and now a vocal disability which is preventing me from singing professionally.

Many times I was ready to give up, but I did not. I thought of re-entering the business world and forgetting about being a cantor, and once I came very close. So far, each and every time I am ready to quit, I get a sign, my decision to become a cantor is somehow validated, and I find myself in another synagogue. It took me a very long time to learn certain aspects of the profession—much longer than the education I received. They did not teach us how to maneuver the politics of a synagogue. Coming out of the for-profit sector of business did not fit the non-profit milieu I am now immersed in. For instance, one Midwestern synagogue I served cited this reason for not renewing my contract: I was an aggressive Israeli-New Yorker—that is, I was too direct! Most Israelis I know are just like me. I am not diplomatic enough and, having lived my early days in a communist environment, I have an overdeveloped sense of fairness which is not suitable to synagogue life. Rabbi-cantor relations are not always just and, in reality, they are very different than they were depicted at HUC.

I have learned over the years how to be diplomatic, how to be a good leader through doing, but mostly through teaching. I have also learned how to be less selfish, and how to be more patient and kind. I have learned how to be compassionate and a good listener, and I have given of myself to many people.

Now that I have a vocal disability I did try to re-enter the business world, working part-time at the University of Chicago. That lasted for a few months, and it was a good experience, but it completely confirmed that my place is as a cantor. Doing the holy work that we clergy do every day is the essence of this profession. Even if my voice does not last forever, I know that what I have given to so many these past fourteen years will help them cope with life's mountains. I know that I have made a difference in people's lives, that I have brought them solace from the toils of life's daily hardships. I will keep finding ways to continue to bring that to people. That is what is meaningful to me: to continue to enrich others and to help ensure the continuation of the Jewish people

Maria Dubinsky is a cantor, performer and educator. Born in Moscow, Maria immigrated to Israel in 1990, where she graduated from the Rubin Academy of Music and dance in Jerusalem with a degree in Vocal Performance and Music Education. In 2010 Maria was ordained as a Cantor and received a Masters in Sacred Music from Hebrew Union College – Jewish Institute of Religion in New York City. Since July 2011, Maria serves as a Cantor at Temple Shaaray Tefila in Manhattan.

A performer of classical and Jewish music, Maria Dubinsky has participated in numerous opera productions of the Israeli Opera, as well as in a wide variety of concerts, festivals, recitals, oratorios, chamber ensembles, and opera projects in Israel, Europe and the USA. Since her arrival to New York City in 2006, Maria Dubinsky has served in prayer and song such congregations as Garden City Jewish Center, Union Temple of Brooklyn and North Shore Synagogue in Syosset, NY. Cantor Dubinsky's Master thesis at the Hebrew Union College is focused on Russian and Soviet influences on the development of the Israeli song culture. As a part of her study of the music of the Jews of Russia, Maria regularly performs at the Sidney Krum Concert Series at YIVO Institute for Jewish Research in NY, the Three Sopranos, the Voices of the Mediterranean concert series, Limmud FSU, and more.

Maria is involved in outreach to the Russian-speaking Jewish community in New York City. Cantor Dubinsky is a co-founder of a Russian-Jewish children's theater and runs a program for Manhattan Russian-speakers Firebird/JAR-Ptitsa–Judaism Through Arts in Russian. Maria currently lives in Brooklyn with her husband Arcady and her daughters.

7
Moscow-Tel Aviv-New York
My Search for Identity
Maria Dubinsky

I LIVE IN BROOKLYN AND WORK AT a large Manhattan Reform synagogue. I was born in Moscow and raised in Tel Aviv. Seven years ago, I came to the United States from Israel to pursue my education at the School of Sacred Music at Hebrew Union College–Jewish Institute of Religion. If I were asked to describe my life prior to the decision to become a cantor, I would define it as a roller coaster of immigrations, changes, turns, and spiritual and identity crises. In the course of my life, I've tried myself in numerous professions, but have always returned to my greatest passion: music. After long years of searching and seeking, exploring, failing, and starting over, I finally found the path that made me feel needed, fulfilled, and self-expressed. While remaining a musician, I've discovered a way in which I can help others, fully explore my spiritual potential, and enrich myself.

In this essay, I share my personal story, some aspects of which may not seem directly related to Judaism or the cantorate. Nonetheless, without writing about my life, I wouldn't be able to explain myself properly. Some turbulent events made my spiritual journey a complex one. I feel greatly honored and privileged to be given an opportunity to participate in this project and to share myself with others. But, while speaking openly about my own life, I feel that each of us has a unique story that has the power to move, inspire, and teach. I find great joy in listening to others and I hope that you will find my sharing interesting as well.

People often ask me what made me pursue the career of a Jewish professional. Today I feel that my decision to become a cantor was inevitable, considering the events that I have gone through. Since I was a little girl, I sensed that things could not operate merely by the laws of physics and that there must have been some bigger power that drove our lives. In other words, although back then I could not verbalize this assertion, I have always believed in God. However, the essential right of religious freedom was taken from me by the realities of Soviet life. Religious practices of all denominations were considered "the opiate for the masses" and were strictly forbidden by the government. Being Jewish in the Soviet Union was not easy either. It often meant being "different" or the "other." Anti-Semitism became such an integral part of the governing policy that it was often accepted by the Jews themselves as an inseparable part of their lives.

But prior to discussing my Jewish upbringing, I would like to touch on some of the circumstances under which my personality was formed first in the USSR, then in Israel, and later in the United States of America.

Moscow
Survival, Character Building, Emergence of Identity

I was born in the heart of Moscow, the capital of the Former Soviet Union. The oldest of three, I grew up as a reflective and dreamy child who lived in her own world and was not always connected to the surrounding reality. My mother was a painter and my dad was a computer engineer who did not care much about his profession. Instead, he was loyally devoted to music. He did not receive formal music education as a child, but at the age of sixteen, after my grandmother made the mistake of buying him a record of the famous Russian bass Fyodor Chaliapin, he became violently infected by the singing virus, which shaped the course of his—and ultimately my—entire life. When at work, my father spent most of his time learning music theory, harmony, and sight-reading. As a child, I was surrounded by music, visual arts, and heated anti-Soviet discussions held at the kitchen in the best tradition of the Russian intelligentsia. When I was four years old, my parents were unprecedentedly lucky to obtain a separate small one-bedroom apartment at the center of Moscow. Housing was a big issue in the Soviet Union. Often a few families had to share one apartment with common utilities and kitchen. But we got an apartment of our own and, although it was small and overcrowded by my parents, the three of us, a dog, and a cat, I felt that we lived in a palace. After all, children see everything with different eyes and manage to derive the best out of almost any situation. It's a shame that this view of life disappears as we grow older.

I was a quiet and lonely child, always making something up, dreaming, pondering. I felt remote and separated from the world around me. I did not have much energy and preferred to spend my time reflecting and observing rather than acting and playing. As it soon became clear to my parents, social interaction with peers did not come easy to me. I did not have the natural gift of befriending the children around me. Although trying my best, I was lacking the skills that so many kids intuitively had. And, yet, being a part of the society was tremendously important to me. Despite being painfully shy, quiet, and introverted, I desperately sought to make friends. But lively and energetic children did not care much for a quiet girl with an overly vivid imagination. I ended up having a couple of strong friendships, none of which were in school. At school what I faced was abuse and despair.

My mom blamed all of my social fiascos on the fact that we were Jewish. "It's because the children's parents are anti-Semitic," she said. It was always the same: "I suffered from anti-Semitism, your father did, and you will too. It's inevitable." Well, anti-Semitism was surely a part of it, but there was more. I was simply different from most of my peers. The anti-Semitism was obvious, though, and often the first spark would be kindled by the teacher, who would urge the students not to be friends with "this Jewish girl."

Not only were my parents Jewish, but they were also staunchly anti-Soviet. "Never share with anyone the things we say at home," they conveyed to me over and over again. Starting at a very early age, I felt I was part of some conspiracy: a Jewish girl (you couldn't really hide that), who also needed to be very secretive about what she heard at home. I didn't really understand why listening to *Voice of America* and cursing the Soviet regime was so top secret, but I enjoyed playing according to my parents' rules. Conspiracy, mystery, and a hidden longing for adventure; these were probably the reasons for my love of detective stories and the dream to become a prominent militia detective.

It seems to me that the intense Jewish awareness of my parents led them to be "actively Jewish" in one of the few ways available to them: by being anti-Soviet. It was another way for them to rebel against the oppressive Soviet regime. There were numerous Jews in the Soviet Union and everyone knew who they were, since nationality—the fifth point, as it was called back then—was indicated in all documents of at least some significance. If you did not have a Jewish last name, were blonde, and had a small nose and, most of all, if you somehow managed to fix the fifth point and listed you as Russian, you were lucky. But if you were unable to get rid of your Jewish last name, if you had black hair, dark eyes, a "Jewish" nose, and did not address the notorious fifth point, you were at a major disadvantage. Jews experienced difficulties getting accepted to good schools, universities, prestigious jobs, etc. Discrimination was everywhere, and was a semi-open policy of the government. That is why if you were Jewish and wanted to succeed, you had to be better than the best. And, considering the fact that so many Jews managed to hold leading positions in numerous spheres of Soviet life, they were clearly successful at being the best.

Understandably, many Jews were ashamed of their upbringing and tried to conceal it. They declared themselves Russians and rejected anything that would remind them of their Semitic roots. Not so my parents, the proud Jews and Zionists. Practicing Judaism was almost impossible in the realms of Soviet life. To be fair, I must mention that practicing any religion, not just Judaism, was challenging and even dangerous. My father spent over ten years singing in a church choir. This was another thing I could not share with my peers. Feeling outcasts as Soviet citizens and cherishing the tradition of their ancestors, my parents, despite the danger of being arrested, did all they could in order to introduce us to Judaism and its customs. My mother kindled Shabbat candles and tried to make us aware of some basic laws of *kashrut*.

Once a year, on Simchat Torah, we even went to a synagogue located not far from our house. I didn't understand the significance of the holiday, and yet whatever I saw filled me with a sense of awe. I intuitively felt that I was a part of something fundamentally important. The gathering at the synagogue was more than just celebrating a holiday. It was a protest, an expression of national awareness in the midst of oppression. The uninhibited childish joy that I could read on the faces of young and old Jews was a celebration of freedom, a statement of liberation, and victory over the regime. Could these people be arrested? Yes, they could and sometimes were. But they could not care less.

Today, thirty years later, I know what Simchat Torah is about. I am a female cantor who celebrates all of the Jewish holidays. I am the one who leads them. But I've never experienced the same awe and joy that I felt watching those old men dancing with the Torah in the small old synagogue in Moscow.

It is to my mother's credit that, as opposed to so many other Jews, we did not try to hide our nationality. Embarrassed, yes. Since I was very young, I remember the embarrassment and the sense of being a second-class person, but I always knew that I had to be proud of who I was. And that's exactly how I felt: embarrassed and proud. My mom made a big deal out of celebrating Shabbat. She looked out the window to check for the three first stars and then we kindled the candles—without the blessing, *challah*, or wine, but with a sense of great significance.

I would like to touch on my school years in Moscow just a little bit more. It was a gloomy period of my life, but it was what formed my personality and largely made me who I am today.

School was not fun. Most of the subjects went by me as though I was not present in class. I think I had some serious undiagnosed learning disabilities. (Today, I can proudly say that I overcame them all and am capable of learning everything I want fast and efficiently.) While at school, I was mostly dreaming or drawing. My notebooks were filled with multiple drawings of people, fashion styles, stories, and more. In my dreams, I always imagined myself being a teacher. Starting sometime around fourth grade, the girls of my class chose me as a subject of bullying. What started as mild teasing turned into a real problem. My life became miserable and I came home crying every day. My mother refused to enroll me in a different school. "You have to live through this. Otherwise, it will start again," she said. I persevered with many tears and some suicidal thoughts. The abuse stopped after two years, shortly after a movie about a bullied teenage girl made a deep social impact in Russia. My mother came to school and had a conversation with my offenders. "Did you watch the movie?" she asked. "Yes," replied the girls. "Did you feel sorry for the main heroine?" "Yes." "So why do you do the same thing to someone else?" And, just like that, it stopped. A single conversation discontinued two years of severe bullying. I did not become more popular, but the abuse became more passive aggressive and less overt.

Why do I choose to write about this? There are several reasons. First, the experience made me realize that never again would I let anyone treat me that way. Second, it made me stronger. But, most importantly, as a role model and a spiritual leader, I can use the experience to educate teenagers, both the bullies and those who feel like outcasts. It so happens that I have a chance to do this at my work quite often and with great success. I know exactly what abused kids are going through, which helps me earn their trust and establish a relationship with them. On the other hand, sharing my experience with the bullies helps them understand their victims' feelings firsthand.

When I was twelve years old, two of my classmates invited me to join a French language chorus they were part of. That experience completely transformed my life. For the very first time, I felt that I belonged to a community of equals where people didn't mock me, but treated me with respect. The chorus became the biggest joy of my life. I had found new friends. I was accepted and greatly enjoyed it, and I realized that nothing causes me more satisfaction than singing. When I sang, I felt fully and completely happy. After migrating to Israel, I observed that many of my immigrant teen friends were deeply invested in theater. It occurred to me how important it is for lost teenagers to find a secure haven that will nurture them and elevate their self-esteem.

My parents spoke about immigrating since I was very young. They hated the Soviet country and would do anything it took to leave it behind. After the Perestroika hit in 1985, the promise of immigration became real. At the end of the 1980s, Moscow's

Jewish population was stirring. On the one hand, Jews were talking about and preparing for immigration, all the while trying to keep their apartments and summer houses, buying, selling, inquiring, hoping, fearing, daring, staying, leaving, wishing. On the other hand, people all over were discussing upcoming pogroms that were about to strike. An anti-Semitic organization named Pamiat (Memory) was believed to be the force behind the anti-Jewish sentiment that infested Russia at the time. Fearing the pogroms, my parents, who were normally very tolerant and trusting of my judgment, forbade me from returning home late and walking outside on my own. As it turned out, the rumors about pogroms did not materialize, but they caused many Jews to migrate. Initially my family wanted to move to the United States, but my uncle, a young Zionist, refused to go anywhere but Israel. Then, after 1989 the United States temporarily stopped accepting new immigrants from the Soviet Union. So we made *aliyah* to Israel.

Tel Aviv
Formative Years, Loss of Faith, and Identity Crisis

I, who for the first time in my life had found the niche where I belonged, refused to immigrate. I was thirteen years old—a difficult age to leave your life behind and start over. I begged my parents to leave me in Moscow with my grandparents. This, of course, didn't work, and on March 5, 1990, I found myself crying at the Sheremetyevo international airport.

We had to pay the government in order to give up our Soviet passports. We also had to leave everything behind. Starting in 1991, after the fall of the USSR, people could privatize their real estate, but we literally lost everything we had.

My parents didn't care. They couldn't wait to leave the country that made them feel so oppressed. We separated from our family and friends and left on a plane that was routed to bring us to our historic homeland. Someone asked me recently what I remember from my immigration. I remember a sense of finality—the realization of the fact that we were leaving for good without the hope of return. When kissing my paternal grandparents goodbye, I was not sure whether I would see them again. I wasn't even sure whether I'd be able to call them. The feeling was paralyzing. I froze in one spot without being able to move. How could I leave the people and places I loved, friends, relatives, my home, neighborhood—my entire life—everything that mattered to me in the world? Silently, with tears in my eyes, I proceeded to the plane.

We flew through Bucharest, Romania. The only thing I remember from there is being amazed at how far one could get with a bribe. That was also how it worked in Russia, but my parents never gave bribes (and as a result we never had anything). In Bucharest, however, my parents were prepared with a few bottles of vodka in their handbag. Those bottles had a great effect and opened many doors for us at the Romanian airport.

And then we were headed for Ben Gurion Airport in Israel. The flight was overbooked and I was overwhelmed by everything I saw. I was captivated by an olive that was served to us as part of our airplane meal. That was the most exotic food I had ever tasted.

Israel greeted us with short palm trees—which seemed totally surreal after Moscow's snow and bare winter trees—and a warm, thick tropic smell that surrounded me everywhere I went. Today, when I think of Israel, I think of that smell. We received a goody bag with a little food and some treats from the Department of Immigration, and the taxi took us to the south of Tel Aviv, where our friends rented us an apartment. We were wearing funny Russian coats and weird snow boots—the best of our Moscow attire. Israel's March was far too warm for that, but that was basically all we had—our luggage was lost during the lengthy flight. Without having even clean underwear, we were close to panicking.

Two hours after arriving at our new home, we heard a knock on the door. "Do you have new immigrants here?" boomed a loud male voice. "We've brought some stuff for them to wear." I didn't understand what he said, of course, but his actions spoke better than his words. The man unloaded three huge bags, looked critically around the room, welcomed us, and left. The bags were filled with clothes. After years of constant searches for non-Soviet clothing, I thought that I was in heaven. My friends in Russia would die of envy. There were many articles in those bags, but I lost my speech upon seeing an almost-new pair of Levi's jeans. Israel wasn't so bad after all. My loftiest dream had finally come true.

Israeli people appeared to be loud and restless and were sometimes rude and overbearing. They were also extremely warm and empathetic—in spite of their loud and anxious ways, they were always there for you. It took me time to learn to appreciate Israelis, and I must say that I miss them dearly here in New York City.

I was enrolled in the eighth grade at a local high school, as I also attended *ulpan* to learn Hebrew. *Ulpan* was fine, but school . . . The goal of the program was to gradually integrate immigrant kids into the school environment. First we attended school once a week and *ulpan* the remaining four days. Then it was two days of school, three, and so on, until no *ulpan* remained. The cultural shock was immense. It was the very beginning of the Great Aliyah from the Soviet Union and Russian immigrants were still a novelty. While my classmates were kind to me, I felt like I was a trained talking monkey. I was scared and confused by the awfully free behavior of my classmates that seemed unreal compared to the strict discipline of the Soviet Union. I felt that I was an alien who fell from the moon.

Luckily, an *ulpan* friend told me about a high school for the arts in Tel Aviv and I was accepted to the music department. On the first of September I started ninth grade. I feared that my new classmates would jump out of windows and run through the classroom the same way students at my previous school had done. To my great surprise, after the teacher entered the classroom, everyone stood up and greeted her. Just like we did back in Moscow. This was a great relief. The school, Ironi Alef in Tel Aviv, was the gift that I was granted for all of the suffering I had experienced in Russia. Although I didn't speak Hebrew well, I felt that everyone was speaking my language. I first shared a class with actors and visual artists, and then just with the theater department. Despite the fact that I made new friends and school was fascinating, I still longed for my friends and family in Moscow. A troubled teenage immigrant, I was confused, timid, shy, and insecure. To give some credit to my new classmates, they were incredibly supportive and understanding. Due to their kind and respectful presence, I soon started to come out of my shell. But the best thing was that now, during school time, I could engage in what I loved most: music.

Shortly after coming to Israel, I realized that I wanted to be an opera singer. That realization came to me out of the blue at a music camp where I spent the summer months after making *aliyah*. I was coming from a choir rehearsal with a group of girls. One of them asked what we wanted to become when we grew up. Everyone said something. When it was my turn, I confidently replied: "I'm going to become an opera singer." This was weird since I had never thought about becoming an opera singer before, but when the words came out of me, I knew that my destiny has been decreed. From that moment, my entire life became a journey toward becoming an opera singer.

While greatly enjoying my school and my new friends, one issue left me perplexed. My family came to Israel at the very beginning of the Great Aliyah. At that time, "Russian" students were in the minority and I was mainly making friends with the "Israeli" children. Before long, Russian-speakers started to flood Tel-Aviv and my social circles started to switch. One thing was common to Russian and Israeli teenagers: both groups seemed to be quite anti-religious. After my Jewishly oppressed childhood, Zionist parents, and anti-Semitic experiences, I had an idealistic notion of being able to practice Judaism freely and proudly in the Holy Land. In my own terms, this meant celebrating Shabbat and Jewish holidays, keeping kosher, learning about Jewish traditions. I did not intend to become Orthodox-religious, but sought to remain respectful and mindful of my Jewish upbringing. It seemed natural finally being able to celebrate my Judaism in Israel. Nonetheless, after making *aliyah*, my family and I became "Russians" or "Stinky-Russians," as many locals would call us. I was lucky to get into a very good school, though my younger siblings did not and were exposed to some xenophobic expressions. What surprised me the most was the fact that my liberal peers from the center of Tel Aviv did not observe any Jewish traditions. They bragged about eating pork, not observing any of the festivals and not being interested in learning Jewish religious literature or history. This attitude was widely held by my "Russian" friends.

Judaism was such a foreign part of the Soviet reality that adjusting to these new Jewish concepts seemed difficult and often unnecessary. It was hard enough for me to be a young immigrant, but losing everything my parents made me believe in was particularly difficult. I started to ask myself questions that I hadn't asked before. Who was I? Was I "Russian"? Should I be ashamed of myself for believing in God and wanting to observe Jewish holidays? Eventually, my spiritual self-awareness dove into serious crisis, but I was aware that this time I would not be able to move to another country in order to solve it. Israel was the desirable destination where Jewish people could openly build their Jewish identities, and if I couldn't get it in Israel, there was no hope left for me anywhere. As opposed to my musical training, where everything was clear and comprehensible, I struggled to find myself. The more I thought about it, the more intense my inner conflict became.

Shortly after coming to Israel I realized that I desperately needed a change. In order to live and evolve I could not continue being the dreamy and inert girl that I used to be. My world was changing and I needed to upgrade my personality in accordance with it. One night, before sunset, I was sitting in my room and it occurred to me. I saw in front of me two clear choices: to remain the way I was, and grow to be a weak and helpless person who blames all of her failures on circumstances, or start transforming. I knew instantly that transformation would not be easy and could take years. But I also knew that it would give me the opportunity to finally take charge of my life. This was a turning point: at that moment, I started the process of self-establishment and life-long identity building. This process, which started twenty-three years ago, I dare to hope, will not end as long as I'm alive.

High school passed and then the army. The two years I spent in the IDF service where formative in establishing me both socially and emotionally. I was offered a chance to become an officer in the army and continue with a military career, but I was not willing to give up music and singing, and so declined.

After being demobilized, I returned to Moscow to study vocal performance. The Moscow that just a couple of years prior seemed so appealing was now foreign and even hostile. I struggled to make a living. People on the streets were rude and uncaring. Worst of all was that the connection I shared with my childhood friends was lost. I was once told that after you serve in the IDF, you develop a deep sense of belonging to Israel. That was exactly what happened to me. Seven years after leaving Russia, I was longing for Israel in the same way I sought to return to my home town just a few years earlier.

Coming back to Israel was an important landmark in my life. In 1990, I was brought there by my parents against my will. Seven years later, returning to Israel was my own choice. Russia was foreign. Israel was home. I had fully accepted it as my land. I learned to appreciate its beauty and its challenges, its controversies, its sincere, open, and sometimes rude people, its humid and lazy heat, the sweet tropic smell of its flowers. I embraced its noises, smells, sights—everything. I was so happy to finally find a home. At last I found some inner peace.

I enrolled in the Music Academy in Jerusalem, studying in the vocal performance and education departments. It was an engaging and busy time. In order to pay tuition and sustain myself financially, I explored numerous professions. I became a professional translator and worked at leading Russian-language Israeli newspapers and magazines. Later on, I went to study professional jewelry design and for a short time tried my skills as an apprentice jeweler at a small factory. I studied foreign languages, engaged in visual arts, but mostly I sang. I was proud of myself for always having numerous musical gigs. It was very important for me to not only study music, but to also make a living from it.

At the beginning of the twenty-first century, my parents "won" green cards and moved to the United States. My father, a singer himself, studied *hazzanut*, and was pursuing a cantorial career in America. My parents started the process of *t'shuvah* a few years prior to that, while still in Israel. As I mentioned earlier, my mother always sought to become more observant. As it is not an easy process for a secular person, especially for someone who grew up in the former Soviet Union, far from religion, it took my mother many years before she stopped traveling and answering phone calls on Shabbat and started being strictly kosher. After my father began studying *hazzanut*, he also started to observe the *mitzvot*: the obligations of Jewish law.

Meanwhile, I remained in Israel, got married, and worked hard pursuing a carrier as an opera singer. My professional path knew ups and downs, but making it as an opera soloist in Israel was challenging and I often felt unfulfilled. What made it more difficult was that every time I spoke with my parents, they tried to convince me to keep Shabbat and pray three times a day. They claimed that as soon as I started, all of my troubles would disappear. I was an obedient daughter and I tried my best, but I simply could not commit to what my parents urged me to do. After living in Israel for many years, the general concept of "all or nothing"—being very Orthodox or completely secular—became engrained in me. To this day, I struggle with this Israeli black-and-white approach.

While in this professional crisis, I turned to my parents for consolation. My parents, in their turn, used the opportunity to impose a strictly religious lifestyle on me. As I wrote at the beginning of this chapter, I've always believed in God. But, interestingly enough, the more I tried to follow my parents' advice—to pray regularly from the *siddur*, not to travel on Shabbat, etc.—the more I felt my genuine faith fading away. I was forcing myself to pray and tried to enjoy something that I really hated, until my faith, which used to be the most natural part of my being, disappeared. I learned that authentic faith could not be forced. This was quite an unpleasant sensation. I felt the ground moving under my feet and I didn't have anything to hold on to. Ironically, instead of strengthening my spiritual and religious awareness, as my parents hoped I would, I lost my belief.

This was a difficult time. My singing career was in decline. Israel was in major financial turmoil, which sabotaged most of my musical and other freelance engagements. On top of everything, I didn't know who I was anymore. I desperately sought some kind of spiritual growth, but I struggled. Most of all, I felt that my potential, both professional and human, was tremendously unfulfilled. I needed to create, do, give, evolve; but I was in a place where I couldn't do any of that. I was miserable and in an existential crisis. What I wanted most was to run away to some place where no one knew me. My husband, Arcady, was my greatest comfort and support. He was and still is the foundation that keeps me together.

Another source of inspiration was my engagement in visual arts of different kinds. I was making jewelry, sculpting, painting, and crafting anything that would satisfy my unrestrained creativity. Work with clay, metals, stones, wood, and other natural materials made me feel more centered. I could take the materials of the earth and make from them something with my own hands, which meant that I could create and give the universe something tangible and real. My desire to create was so strong that I had no choice but to find ways to satisfy it.

New York
An Unexpected Turn, Becoming a Cantor, and Reinventing Spiritual Identity

My father kept urging me to apply to a cantorial school. I was always puzzled by how, although being Orthodox, he was never opposed to me becoming a cantor. He was, in fact, the driving force that pushed me towards it. I really did not want to become a cantor. The only thing I cared about was my opera career. Besides, I was in the middle of a major identity crises. I needed to settle my life and was not ready to make it more complicated than it already was.

Then things became really bad. I felt that doors were being shut in my face, one after another, and there wasn't much left for me to do in a lazy and crowded Tel Aviv. One day, after coming home from a particularly embarrassing gig, I had a revelation. I was sitting near the piano and it dawned on me that I had reached my lowest point. From there, I could only start to rise. And then I suddenly knew exactly what I needed to do. My thoughts were clear and my mind was determined. "Go call the cantorial school," said a little but confident voice in my head. And I obeyed. I followed that little voice, which to me meant that becoming a cantor was a calling from above.

When I started to attend first-year cantorial classes at the Hebrew Union College-Jewish Institute of Religion (HUC) in Jerusalem, I didn't know anything about cantors, Jewish liturgical music, Torah cantillation or *nusach*. Moreover—and this scared me more than anything else—I didn't know anything about Americans, who made up the student body (HUC is an American institution that has its first-year clergy courses in Jerusalem). Although the cultural shock was great, the musical adjustment was much easier. When I first heard cantorial students learning cantillation and chanting prayers, I started to cry. It was a true revelation: I felt that I had returned home after a long journey. Somehow, while the students were chanting, I knew exactly what should come next. Without ever hearing those melodies before, I knew them. The same thing happened a few years later in a class of Yiddish folk and art songs. I wasn't familiar with any of the songs, but somehow I knew them on a very profound level. Call it genetic memory or something else, but there is something hidden in us Jews that we carry inside for generations, without even knowing it. That is, until it wakes up and bursts out.

After a few months of studying English, going through extensive interviews and exams, and making myself familiar with the specifics of American Reform Judaism, I was accepted to the cantorial department at HUC. I was supposed to finish the first year in Israel, and then relocate to New York City. That year in school was tremendously interesting, informative, and diverse. Every day I discovered something new about Jewish liturgy, history, or Jewish music. And each time it seemed as though I knew this stuff already, but had forgotten it. Genetic memory . . .

My identity crisis gradually started to disappear. Everything started to make sense. I realized that all of the spiritual turbulences I went through in the period between my *aliyah* to Israel and the relocation to the United States were essential steps on my way to self-exploration. I needed to go through the searches, despairs, disappointments, and resentment of religion in order to emerge and reappear as a spiritually mature human being. Everything happened for a reason, and I needed to reach my lowest point, lose my faith, move to another country, and go through five years of a seminary to become a *hazzan* and a leader in a Jewish community. Applying to cantorial school, along with marrying my husband and giving birth to my daughter, was the best thing that ever happened to me. It opened the world to me and made me a better person. Indeed, this profession continues to make me a better person every day.

After finishing my first year in Israel, my husband and I left for New York. The first couple of years in the U.S. were very difficult. I came to America in the seventh month of pregnancy, so as I was becoming a new mother, I also studied full time, learned English, and supported my family economically since my husband didn't have a work permit. Gradually, our life became more manageable and we no longer had to struggle to survive. I was blessed with a beautiful class. Throughout my five years of cantorial school, I felt the powerful support and empathy of my classmates. I loved being in school. The program was demanding and the English language was tough, but my natural curiosity and strong thirst for knowledge enabled me to study with great intensity.

One of the main challenges I faced in school and still face in my career is the fact that, after living in Israel for sixteen years, the concept of keeping "all or nothing" had strongly impacted me. Although I am liberal and open-minded, I found myself struggling with some concepts of Reform Judaism, which at times seemed to me almost too liberal. I must say that my Orthodox parents, who were then living in Brooklyn, were surprisingly accepting of what I was doing and appeared to be proud of me. My father was serving as a *ba'al t'fillah* in an Orthodox synagogue in South Brooklyn. The two of us compared the *nusach*, modes, and melodies that we used in our synagogues for different occasions. We discussed *nusach* in the exact same way as we had talked about our work in the New Israeli Opera just a few years earlier. I loved these "professional" discussions and valued them highly. In their Orthodox community, my parents bragged about how their daughter was studying to become a Reform cantor until a few of their friends stopped talking to them. My naïve mother couldn't believe that the reason for this was the profession of their daughter.

Studying in a Reform seminary while being exposed to an Orthodox environment was hard. I needed to find my own expression of Judaism that didn't have to be Reform, Conservative, or Orthodox. I needed to find who I was as a Jew. My liturgy teacher at HUC in Israel once said something that deeply resonated with me. When I wrote a journal entry about my fear of not being able to fit into some of the realms of the Reform movement, she replied that although I was entering Reform Judaism, I was going to become a *cantor*, and that the definitions of Reform, Conservative, or whatever else were not as important. It was more about how I shaped my cantorate and what gifts I could bring to the people around me. She was right. I was becoming a cantor and I needed to find my own niche where I could rise above denominational limits and feel self-expressed spiritually, musically, and religiously.

Another challenge that I came across at the beginning of my career was my strong and genuine desire to dig deeper, to learn more, and to explore Judaism on a more profound level. Not having much prior knowledge, I felt tremendously ignorant: the more I learned, the less I realized that I knew. How could I compare myself to those who grew up with Judaism and who were exposed to deep expressions of Jewish living since childhood? Even today, when I need to teach something, I often feel that I'm cheating, pretending to be more knowledgeable than I actually am. When this does happen, I am transparent. My congregants see that I don't know it all. So what? I'm not embarrassed to admit when I don't know something. Why should I pretend that I'm something that I'm not? I'm not perfect, and I do not strive for perfection. I strive for growth and learning. I want to learn and to know more. Will I ever be satisfied with the level of my knowledge? Of course not. How boring my life would become if I knew it all! So, when I feel "ignorant," I don't hesitate to sincerely share it with my congregants. They truly appreciate my sincerity.

Another thing: my intense, though relatively brief, experience as a cantor has taught me that nowadays there is a tendency to simplify and lighten up the content of whatever we present to our congregants. This applies to many spheres of congregational life, such as worship, liturgy, education, and music. In my opinion, we often try to present things as happy, light, easy, fun, and upbeat as we possibly can. God forbid if we challenge our congregants intellectually or musically and provide them with too much food for thought. To me, the concept of being always fun comes, at times, at the expense of compromising the quality and the content of the material we present. My general feeling is that we sometimes lack substance. Substance is all I personally care about. When we come to a synagogue, we want to feel, to get elevated, to experience something that moves our souls. Such feelings are hard to attain without being exposed to the "real thing," getting to the "core," or "touching the nerve." I do not suggest that we need to become too gloomy or overly serious. A healthy sense of humor and some degree of entertainment are essential companions of synagogue worship. As it seems to me, it's about balance. The balance between making people laugh and provoking them intellectually; between fun, upbeat congregational tunes and inspirational, soulful Jewish music.

I often hear the claim that people do not appreciate serious music anymore. The notion applies to both contemporary Jewish and classical music. I strongly believe that it is not the music we are talking about, but the way it is presented. It's all about putting one's guard down, opening up, taking one's ego out of the picture, and becoming the music, the prayer. Humbleness of the spiritual leader/singer and his or her sincerity, complete openness to the world and to the people around are what create the religious experience. That is when the divine presence, the *Shechinah,* comes down, and that is when we leave the sanctuary moved, touched, and inspired. It does not matter much what music we present. As the Hassidim teach us, every tune is holy. Before I became a cantor, there were instances where I intuitively managed to attain this state of not performing, but *becoming* the music. When that happened, I realized that regardless of how serious or not the repertoire was, everyone in attendance was fully present and engaged. Thus, the cantor can lead liturgy with a simple contemporary folk song or an artistic work of *hazzanut.* The sincerity and soulfulness of the leader are what makes the impact.

After finishing cantorial school in 2010, I struggled to find a job. My husband, little daughter, and I were gradually adjusting to our new life in America, trying hard to battle the nuances of the English language, financial difficulties, small talk, and other unfamiliar codes of American society. While at school, I was serving as a student-cantor at two ideologically and spiritually different synagogues—one on Long Island and one in Brooklyn. They couldn't have been more different, although both belonged to the same movement, both had friendly congregants, and the rabbis of the two synagogues happened to be husband and wife. I had diverse experiences in these two places and felt that I was ready for a real "grown-up" job. Not so easy. Cantorial placement was a disaster. It was a difficult placement year. There were no jobs in New York, and my student visa was about to expire.

When I was almost ready to pack my things and return to Israel, I was offered a job in a synagogue on Long Island. After working there for a year, I was lucky to be accepted as a second cantor at Temple Shaaray Tefila on the Upper East Side of Manhattan, where I happily serve today. My work is intense and fulfilling. I learn and explore new things about myself and my profession every day. At Shaaray Tefila and prior to it, I became greatly involved with the Russian-speaking Jewish community of New York City. After teaching Jewish music and establishing a theater program for Russian-speaking Jewish children, I, along with a colleague from a Conservative synagogue on the Upper West Side of the city, initiated a Russian-Jewish program that takes place regularly at both of our synagogues. Our main goal is to engage the Russian-speaking Jews of Manhattan in synagogue life through arts, music, and intellectual discussions, and to gently connect them to Judaism and Jewish traditions. The participants in the program went through similar experiences as I did: immigration, often as teenagers, discovery of their Jewishness, and the pains of establishing themselves as Russian-speaking American Jews. I experience great satisfaction when leading the program, since I strongly resonate with the people who attend it. Moreover, when I talk to these people, I get to ponder my own Russian-Israeli-American experience over and over again. Every time I do, I discover something new about myself and who I am as a Jew, a Russian-Israeli woman, a musician, and a Jewish clergy member.

What makes this career so special is the connections I manage to create with people. Being there for my congregants, supporting them at times of crisis, and rejoicing with them when things are good. How precious it is! My varied and unusual life has helped me to develop critical thinking and a broad understanding. Sometimes, when being approached by a congregant in distress, I'm unsure whether I'll be able to help. After all, I'm neither a psychologist nor a social worker. But the "right" words somehow come out of my mouth without me even planning what I'm going to say. I wrote before about letting go of one's ego and "becoming the music." The same principle works here: when you put your guard down and let go of your agenda, something larger than yourself comes through, and you know exactly what you need to say. But most of all, you just need to listen and to be present. That is all it takes to make a difference for someone. And, of course, do not hesitate to share yourself. Each of us brings to this world a unique perspective that is tremendously valuable to others. Perhaps, if I had not been bullied at school, if I didn't go through the loss of identity, and didn't struggle to survive financially, I would not be sensitive enough to understand what others are going through. Now, I'm happy to share my own experiences and life lessons with them.

Becoming a cantor has completely and unreservedly changed my life. For a long time, I have felt overwhelmed and a little bit confused— in a good way. My new path constantly pushes me to do things that I never thought I'd be capable of doing. I'm constantly growing, developing, changing, learning, exploring—and this is a gift that I would have never received if I didn't decide to go to a seminary.

I've mentioned more than once that music was my greatest passion, even my obsession. When I was performing music, I was happy, when music wasn't there, I was miserable. Teaching was not an adequate option. I studied music education, but the possibility of becoming a teacher scared me. It was not something I wanted to do or thought I was capable of doing. Today, the biggest part of my job involves different kinds of teaching. Moreover, teaching is the part of my job that I enjoy the most!

After starting my cantorial training, I realized that before an enormous part of my life was missing, and I wasn't even aware of it. The joy of being there for people, making a difference for a student, teaching, working with people of all ages—I could have missed it all. The realization of this fact is what makes me feel so overwhelmed. Obviously, my passion for music did not disappear. Music is my life: it is what nurtures my soul and inspires me for growth. Discovering the immensely rich and multifaceted world of Jewish music has made me a better musician. I'm ashamed to admit that prior to starting cantorial school, I was more familiar with the words of a Catholic mass than with any Jewish liturgical texts. That was simply the nature of my work as a classical singer. Today I'm tremendously grateful for the circumstances of my life that brought me to cantorial school and changed me forever.

I am delighted that I can give my six-year-old daughter the gift of being able to freely form her national, religious, and spiritual identity. It does not matter to me what she will decide to become in the future. What I care about is the fact that I can provide her with the necessary tools that will allow her to choose her own way to be Jewish. I greatly enjoy watching her reciting the *Sh'ma* before going to bed. I admire and encourage her engagement in learning the language of her people and exploring its history. As someone who for many years was not permitted to believe in God or to express my religiosity the way I wanted to, I tremendously appreciate the freedom of religion that I have finally managed to attain.

From Moscow to Tel Aviv to New York, my journey has brought me to the place I am now. This reflection, which is the recitation of my personal story, speaks about the emergence, development, and establishment of my spiritual identity and my evolution as a person, musician, teacher, and Jew. I'm tremendously grateful for each and every piece of the experience God provides me with and, most of all, I'm thankful for the lessons I learn. After years of searching, I've managed to salvage my faith and regain my religion, but the cycle is not completed. This is just the beginning of the great adventure called "life," and I cannot wait to see what gifts and challenges it will bring me next.

Cantor Galit Dadoun-Cohen brings a unique voice to the cantorate, combining a diverse Jewish background and extensive musical training. Born and raised in Ashdod, Israel she earned her Bachelor's of Music and Artist Diploma from the Ruben Academy of Music of Tel Aviv University and her Master's of Music from City University of New York's Brooklyn College. In 2010, she was ordained as Cantor from Hebrew Union College – Jewish Institute of Religion (HUC-JIR). Since then, she has served as the Cantor of Temple B'nai Or in Morristown, NJ.

Galit Dadoun-Cohen has sung opera and classical song in festivals, concerts, and various projects throughout the United States, Europe and Israel. She continues to explore the many realms of Jewish music with various ongoing programs. In her cantorate, she strives to deepen the connection with one's Jewish identity, through music, learning and community building.

During her studies at HUC, Cantor Dadoun-Cohen interned in Temple Shalom in Levittown PA, Temple Sinai in Bayshore, NY, Greenwich Reform Synagogue in Connecticut and her beloved home congregation, Kol Ami in White Plains, NY. Her Master's thesis explored the fusion of traditional Sephardic folk song with Western art music in Jewish music of the 20th and 21st century. She deeply loves contemporary Israeli music, classical music and traditional Eastern European Hazzanut.

Along with her husband Joe, Cantor Galit shares the gratitude and endless joy of raising their three daughters.

8

A PERSONAL EVOLUTION FROM TRADITION TO PROGRESS

Galit Dadoun Cohen

AT WHAT POINT DOES ONE BECOME aware of one's own struggle toward equality and freedom? Is it gradually realized as a heavy burden being carried around? Or does it hit like a ton of bricks, as you realize you've been chained down to misconceptions, unfairness and disparity? Does awareness light up like a light bulb, all of a sudden, like a caricature or cartoon? Or is it achieved slowly through years of self-study, research and reflection? Today, a disparity exists between the status of American and Israeli women in roles of Jewish clergy and leadership. It is hard to believe that the state of Israel, which sits at the cusp of human progress in medicine, computing, military technology and agriculture, can have such regressive views of women's roles in the public practice of Judaism.

Judaism began with the gift of Torah, a treasure that has pioneered a philosophy of fairness and justice. The modern state of Israel was the first to enlist women in the military. In secular Israeli society, women are offered comparatively fair career opportunities and a work environment in which it is manageable to balance the demands of motherhood and full-time work. However, things are quite different when it comes to the practice of Jewish religion, where the government enforces a highly discriminatory rabbinic law that prevents women from practicing Judaism as equal partners with men. This bias does not strictly reside in the government. Much of Israeli society finds it difficult to fathom the idea of women religious leaders.

Childhood in Israel
Growing up in a Traditional Sephardic Family

My own Jewish identity began as a young child, and was part of a seamless tapestry of practically unquestionable principles. I was born in Ashdod, Israel in the early 1970s to two very young North African immigrants—*olim chadashim*. My mother, born in Morocco, was raised in the Jewish ghetto in Rabat, the country's capital. They practiced Judaism traditionally, observed the laws of *kashrut*, and celebrated all the holidays according to customs going back many generations.

My mother immigrated to Israel when she was fourteen, along with her parents and five siblings. Her father—my grandfather— did not survive the hardships of the journey and died on the Mediterranean. The family could not take his body to Israel, and left him behind in a Marseille hospital. A year later they were able to bury him in the holy city of Jerusalem.

This initial interaction with the land and people of Israel made my mother's family's connection to Israel extremely sad and difficult. Upon their arrival in Israel, absorption as new immigrants proved to be quite traumatic. There was a great deal of prejudice directed toward North African immigrants, and work was very hard to find. My grandmother was a grieving young widow who had to raise six children in a strange land whose language she did not know. It was hard to make ends meet, and she sent her two oldest children to find work in France. Today, they are a true family of the Diaspora, spread out across several different countries.

My father was born and raised in Tunisia to a traditional and observant family, and immigrated to Israel a year before he married my mother in 1971. He had lived with his mother and four siblings in France for seven years, and after that he made *aliyah* with his mother and one sister. My father's connection to Israel was strengthened by a childhood of fairly strict Jewish practice and an underground Zionist youth group he attended in Tunisia. For both of my parents, immigration to Israel symbolized a sort of *ge'ula*: redemption from a somewhat persecuted existence as Jews in the Diaspora.

Israel has a history of absorbing hundreds of thousands of immigrants at a time, and the late 1960s and early 70s were no exception. There were waves of immigration to Israel from different countries of North Africa and countries east of the Jordan River such as Iraq, Iran, Syria and Yemen. The Israeli government organized to accommodate them through massive public housing and employment projects. But, despite the state's efforts, immigrants faced much economic adversity. My parents were fortunate enough to find work, but their poverty made it hard to raise a young family and pursue advanced degrees. They knew the importance of education and made considerable sacrifices to ensure that their daughters were all highly educated. Despite the difficult circumstances of immigration, both my parents' families came to Israel with a profound love of the land, and a deep faith in God and Judaism.

My parents are of Sephardic origin, and were raised in Arab countries that were more or less inhospitable to Jews in different periods of history. Sephardic Jews were spread throughout the Ottoman Empire after the Spanish Inquisition and dispersion in 1492. During a period in which much of Europe was hostile to Jews, the Ottoman Empire welcomed them, thinking the Jews would provide positive contributions to its knowledge and labor force. Although Morocco was not part of the Empire, its king was a friend to the Jews through those generations, and allowed an enormous community to grow and thrive.

Sephardic Jews in North African countries lived in gated communities—ghettos—and, for the most part, felt safe and guarded by their governments. In these conditions, they lived with a deep love of Israel and Judaism. Both of my parents shared stories of Zionist yearnings with me, and stories of an often-difficult Jewish life in their home countries. My father's Zionist underground youth group taught them about Israel and Zionism and promised to bring them there someday.

My parents fell in love at first sight and married within a year of meeting each other. They had French culture in common—it was prominent in their respective countries—and spoke French to each other and to me when I was young. I learned Hebrew in preschool.

The Judaism I knew growing up was felt most strongly at home. We sat down for Shabbat meals every Friday night and Saturday afternoon and always gathered around for *Kiddush*. Holidays were very joyous family gatherings that involved blessings around the table and lavish meals about which I could write volumes (and excellent cookbooks, too). My father went to synagogue either Friday night or Saturday morning, as well as for the holidays and festivals, but the synagogue did not fully register in my mind as an integral part of practicing Judaism. We rarely attended the synagogue together as a family. Most memorable was during the *N'ilah* service of Yom Kippur and for my grandfathers' *yahrzeits*.

In the synagogue, I sat upstairs with the women or played outside with the other kids. To the best of my recollection, I never questioned why I wasn't allowed to pray downstairs with the men. This was the reality that I knew as a child and everyone followed. I simply dedicated myself to accomplishing the Yom Kippur fast so I could show off at school the next day. It is possible that since I only had sisters, and we were all treated equally, this segregation didn't make a difference to me as a child.

My parents taught us to be curious and ambitious. Study was a Jewish virtue that was firmly passed down to us. I remember my father always saying that we could do anything to which we set our minds, while my mother pushed us to excel at school and did not accept mediocrity. Once I reached the age of twelve, I realized I would not be studying to read from the Torah for my bat mitzvah, but would follow a different path than the boys. It didn't occur to me to question why I was not allowed to read Torah or be upset that I couldn't. I didn't feel like I missed out or lost anything at the time. In those days in Israel, that was not even an option or discussion. I was just grateful to receive a wonderful bat mitzvah gift from my parents. My gift was a trip to Paris and Amsterdam with my mother.

Life in the United States
An Introduction to Reform Judaism

In 1985, the year after my bat mitzvah, our family temporarily moved to Connecticut for my father's work. I studied in the local public school and continued to practice our customs at home. I made a Jewish friend who invited me to visit her Sunday school at the temple. This was my first interaction with American Reform Judaism and it was a powerful cultural shock. I clearly remember one Shabbat dinner. The meal was a huge *challah* sandwich with ham and cheese. I had never before in my life seen non-kosher food, and I was appalled to witness Jewish people eating this forbidden food, at a Jewish gathering! On *Shabbat*! Even the rabbi! This Judaism was different than any Judaism I had ever known. During my teenage years in Connecticut, I learned that there are other ways to practice Judaism and they were very different from what I learned growing up.

In Israel, I was aware of ultra-Orthodox Jews, or *haredim*. On the other hand, I had friends who were very secular and basically did not practice any Jewish religion at home. I could differentiate between "them" and "us" and knew that *haredim* looked different and separated themselves in every aspect of society. Although I didn't know many specifics of their Jewish practice, I did believe they were the guardians of tradition and I was taught to respect them. I admit that I was even a bit scared around them, perhaps because they seemed closed off and the men in that society were not permitted to converse or even look at a woman. Our practice was neither of the two extremes. We were Masorti Jews, which meant we were observant to a certain extent. The more obvious separation that I felt throughout my life growing up was the difference between Sephardim and Ashkenazim, the categorization of Jews according to their heritage or country of ancestry.

Among Sephardim (Jews who trace their ancestry to Spain), there are different levels of observance, and Judaism is practiced to different extents. Ashkenazim (Jews who trace their ancestry to Eastern and Western Europe), are the majority of Jews in

America and are the ones who brought Reform Judaism from Germany in the mid 1800s. I had never seen Reform Jews in Israel, nor did I understand or know of their practices or the philosophy behind the movement.

I continued my curious learning journey attending the religious school. Living in the United States, I transitioned to American culture and American Judaism. I was light years away from practicing or understanding Reform Judaism, but was exposed to it and took part in it socially and culturally. Despite the many differences and how foreign it was to me, I enjoyed being part of it. I enjoyed the community, the closeness, and being among other young Jews in a foreign land. The discussions were a great education for me, getting to know these people and this new Judaism. Of all of the adjustments in my life (another language, new friends, and teenage activities) learning with Reform Jews felt the closest and easiest because I felt part of a people. I was part of a group to which I belonged. Although I was initially judgmental and critical of the movement, I allowed myself to take it all in.

The initial differences seemed strange to me, from the rabbi wearing a robe to the musical instruments in the synagogue. It felt weird that men and women were sitting together, although that was a fairly easy practice to get used to since I enjoyed sitting in the pews with everyone. I did not read into it any deeper meaning of not being treated as a second-class citizen.

The few years we spent living in Connecticut felt like a lifetime to me. We always knew it would be temporary and considered it to be sort of an adventure. I became accustomed to being an American teen with all that it implied. Our Jewish practice at home did not change, and my existence as a Reform Jew was more of a cultural endeavor than a spiritual one. It provided the social outlet that I very much needed, but at no time did I truly identify religiously with the Reform movement. It was "their" practice that I was sharing. In the tenth grade, I was confirmed with the rest of the class and no longer continued to be a part of the local Jewish community. I remained Jewish at home but, by this time, my social life was full of secular activities and I no longer needed to feel Jewish within the community.

Moving Home to Israel

The following year, we returned to Israel and I had to re-adjust to the lifestyle and to a completely contrasting type of high school experience. Once again, it was hard for me to transition to a different way of doing everything, from studying to socializing. Now I was an American in the Israeli system. As a teen, I was much more occupied with my ambition to do well in high school than with my observance of Jewish religion.

As a child growing up in Israel, I didn't think to appreciate the Jewish life around me. I had always taken it for granted because it was simply always there. I didn't have to question my Jewish identity because everyone around me was Jewish. Growing up in the Israeli school system, I didn't appreciate the beauty of studying the biblical stories, the wisdom within those stories, or their reflection on our history and development as a people. The Hebrew language was always at my core, the root of my expression and my identity. Judaism was all around me at all times. Shabbat, the holidays, school—it was in everything. One didn't have to make special mention of it.

The challenge of passing down all that I grew up with to my children has created a deep hole in my stomach. It is a pain that I've taken on by the life choices I have made. I will forever ponder the gains and losses in these choices.

My unusual high school experience of venturing back and forth between two countries segued into a standard Israeli army service experience. In January of 1991, in the midst of the first Gulf war in Iraq, I enlisted in the army like everyone else. I spent the first half of the war enclosed in a sealed room with my immediate family covered by a gas mask. The second half of the war I shared with approximately 200 eighteen-year-old girls going through basic training. We spent quite a few nights together in a sealed room protected by gas masks and terrified. To say the least, *that* was not a "normal" army experience.

As memorable as all of this was, it was short-lived and life went on afterwards. I served my country in a clerical role within occupied Gaza City. Though I did not necessarily learn an important skill during that time, I was given priceless learning experiences that I will never forget. For a certain moment, I was witness to the completely divergent life of our neighbors across the border. It provided a window that has taught me endless life lessons I could not begin to recount, about "us" and "them," about perceptions and misconceptions between two peoples.

Following that service, I began my undergraduate studies in Tel Aviv University as a double major in psychology and music. Over time I immersed myself completely in opera and finally graduated with a bachelor's degree in music and an artist diploma. I was infatuated with the idea of continuing my opera studies in Germany and living in a country that glorifies and promotes opera. The universe unfolded for me in a different direction.

Back to the United States
A Balance of Judaic Practice

Shortly after graduating, I moved to New York City and enrolled in the master's program at the Brooklyn College Conservatory of Music. I was certain this would be another temporary experience and that I would not have to grapple with my long-term identity as a Jewish woman. However, I soon landed my first Jewish job singing in a High Holiday choir and, from there, connected to another opportunity to teach at the Hebrew school at Congregation Kol Ami in White Plains. Once again, I was thrown into circumstances that made me ask enduring Jewish questions. Reform Judaism welcomed me back as an old familiar friend.

In the winter of 2000 I settled down in a Brooklyn apartment and began my studies in the music program at Brooklyn College, City University of New York. I studied with the prestigious Metropolitan Opera singer Mignon Dunn and was very determined to have a career singing opera. I also knew that I definitely wanted to have a family, though I wasn't sure how. Since I had not yet found the love of my life, I focused on becoming a professional singer.

I became attached to Kol Ami and the work I did there with the children. While other things in my life continued to evolve and change, my work within that community was a constant. I learned so much about Judaism in America and the generation of children I taught. I tried to understand the kind of Judaism they experienced at home and realized it was nothing like what I experienced growing up. My connection with my sixth grade students at Kol Ami, and the learning experiences I had in America earlier, taught me so much about American Reform Judaism. It taught me what was important for me as a Jew living in America.

Marriage and Children
Creating a Jewish Home

Two years later, I completed my master's of music degree and met the man of my dreams, with whom I fell in love immediately and am married to today. His Judaism could not have been further from my own. However, one thing that was certain was that we were very passionate toward each other and toward the important goal of having a family and dedicating ourselves to our children.

Even though we were engaged to be married within a few short months, we needed to establish common ground and expectations for our Jewish future together. Despite the fact that we were both Jews, our backgrounds and personal relationships to Judaism were more different than either one of us had anticipated. I grew up in Israel with a very strong sense of Jewish practice in the home and a strong sense of kinship with my fellow Jews in Israel. I embraced the concept of *K'lal Israel*: the whole of Israel and the Jewish people are one large family. But, I did not have the experience of a specific Jewish community or congregation since synagogue was mostly attended by my father. Synagogue affiliation was not a familiar concept in Israel until recent times.

My husband Joe's Jewish background relied mostly on the strength of the Jewish community he experienced during summers at Camp B'nai Brith. He was raised in a remote town in Northern Ontario, Canada, where there were hardly any Jews and, as the years passed, fewer and fewer. Joe's mother, who converted to Judaism to marry his father, worked hard to keep Judaism in the home, but Joe does not have many early memories of Judaism.

In the foreign land of the United States, I was marrying someone with a completely different background and Jewish upbringing. I found myself asking questions I never thought I would ask regarding how to make an appropriate Jewish home. I still find that I am grappling with many issues. My girls continue to ask the most profound questions that bring me to very serious thoughts about their education and future.

The Cantorate
Finding a New Jewish Identity

My Jewish journey in the United States continued to evolve unexpectedly. While teaching at Kol Ami I often had discussions with Cantor Mo Glazman about the possibility of becoming a cantor myself. I knew it was a serious decision, and I could only pursue serving the Jewish people if I did so whole-heartedly.

That year, I was asked by an old friend, Cantor Irena Altshul, if I would sing the High Holiday services while she was away on maternity leave. We knew each other from the music academy in Tel Aviv, where we went to school together. Our paths crossed once again at Temple Israel in New York City. She was a cantor and I was teaching fourth grade in the religious school. I agreed to sing the services, not for a moment thinking of the implications or how the opportunity would alter my life. It turned out to be an extremely beautiful and gratifying experience—one that spoke to me in a very powerful way. As I was singing, I not only felt at ease connecting with the music and the Hebrew prayers but, more importantly, that I was connecting with the people in the room.

I was afforded the gift of sharing beautiful music with a congregation, which was both moving and engaging for me. For the first time in many years, I was singing in my own language—Hebrew—the language in which I express myself most naturally. The texts I was singing were older than any classical text I had sung before, which itself added a whole new level of sacredness. The music and prayers alone were powerful, but I was also singing to a room full of people I knew well: parents, children and families. Although High Holiday music is not necessarily the participatory kind, I felt that I was singing with them. This experience inspired me to become a cantor, and led me to the Hebrew Union College (HUC).

The gift of cantorial school was the answer to almost all my prayers. It enabled me to sing, as I had always dreamed, but in my own language and within a community. As a cantor, I could engage with my audience—I could immerse myself in the teachings I had been doing all those years, but could do so through the medium of music. I could bring my perspective of Judaism from Israel to the American people. I had a newfound duty to Judaism, being close to it and taking part in shaping its future. Through my relationship with the Reform movement, I knew that my own practice, although different, would be tolerated, welcomed and cherished. The movement always welcomed me into its arms, but I had previously only been a visitor, without really being fully part of it. It was only the following year, in the most extremely unfortunate circumstances, that I finally adopted it as my own philosophy.

My husband and I had experienced hardship as a young couple. Around the time I made the decision to attend the cantorial school at HUC, I happily became pregnant. I carried the pregnancy full term and could not imagine the tragic outcome that was to come. Through a series of complications during labor, our little boy, the promise of our future as a family, did not survive. He died after only two days of life on this planet. We named him Ethan.

I found myself not knowing how to cope with such tragedy. I had my very close family and my wonderful friends to help me through this, and help they did. But there is nothing on earth that prepared me for a loss of that proportion. Although I was with Ethan for a mere two days, I felt the full tragedy of losing a child. Almost instinctively, I turned to Judaism to guide me through the grieving process. In the hospital the most incredible chaplains connected us with the right people: the cemetery, a *mohel* for an optional *bris*, and counselors. The pain was great but we needed to "do" many things. Since I had undergone an emergency Caesarian section, there were many health restrictions upon me that limited my abilities and movement.

I wanted to follow the Jewish traditions and was hoping to receive the correct tools to help me overcome the worst tragedy I had ever experienced. I was grateful to have Judaism to aid me through it, and to give me some sort of closure. The chaplains in the hospital tried to counsel me on how to go about the procedures in the coming days given my health limitations. Within hours, my distant relatives offered an entire set of unsolicited advice and restrictions according to Judaism for this type of situation. They expressed a strong prohibition on having a funeral and especially having the mother of the baby attend. They said it was forbidden in Judaism to have a funeral for a baby that lived for less than thirty days and that the mom should not attend since it would be bad luck.

I couldn't believe that Judaism would give such terrible instructions, so I called my dearest rabbi of Kol Ami, Shira Milgrom. I told her of what I had heard, asked what was permitted *halachikally* (according to Jewish law), and hoped to hear her wisdom. She corrected the misconception saying there is no such *halachah* (Jewish law) that restricted having a funeral for a baby that lived under thirty days. She clarified that Judaism does not obligate a funeral for such cases. In earlier times, it was more common for babies to die in childbirth, and the dismissal of the obligation was meant to protect parents from having many recurring painful experiences. However, in modern societies, since such a tragedy is not common, it is recommended to take part in a ritual to help the grieving process. She also added that there is no restriction for the mother to attend such a funeral.

A second pressure was to perform the burial "as quickly as possible." Since Ethan died early Friday morning, it was a "*mitzvah*" to bury him before *Shabbat*. But I could not be dismissed from the hospital to attend the ceremony that day and the thought of waiting until Sunday was scandalous. Still, I felt very strongly about properly departing from my baby and I was not about to give up.

For the first time in my life, I was grateful and honored to identify with the Reform philosophy of making an informed choice. In the hardest and darkest place of my life, I wanted the freedom to grieve my own way, from a spiritual place, and a place deemed healthy by modern psychologists. I did not want my decisions dictated to me by ancient law, or by superstitions that had been passed down as law. I wanted Judaism to be there for me and not the other way around. I wanted to experience traditional Judaism through the lens of modernity. Ethan's short life made my traditional and Reform worlds collide.

My father had a very hard time with all of this, and was in so much pain himself that he didn't really know how to handle the situation. Threats were thrown around about what I was allowed and not allowed to do, and while my mom felt pressure from both directions, she powerfully stood by me, supporting my decisions to grieve the way I chose. After a lot of crying, my father shared with me that it broke his heart that he couldn't take the pain away from me, that he couldn't make it better for his own child. I suppose he didn't have enough tools of his own to cope with the loss either.

We buried Ethan in Roosevelt Memorial Park in Philadelphia and had a ceremony led by my dearest friend, Cantor Guy Bonne. Both Joe and I wrote our personal words to Ethan. The ceremony was attended by many friends and family who came to hold our hand. At the end, Joe and I spent a few moments alone at the grave, crying together until we could no longer. Every year, we visit Ethan's grave and I will forever be grateful to Rabbi Shira for enabling this memory to be part of my life, as well as having the physical place I can go to remember my baby. This trial brought

Joe and me closer together and taught my entire family a lesson about life and about Judaism.

I continued on to cantorial school with the full support and tremendous pride of both of my parents. If I had doubted about going in the right direction, I now fully believed that I was in the right place. The following fall, I picked up the pieces of my soul and began my studies at HUC. By that point I had overcome my own judgments of traditional Judaism and completely reconciled with the Reform Judaism I had come to appreciate and respect.

Looking Ahead
Women and Judaism

For years, it was as though I had two personalities and two Jewish identities: the one who grew up in Israel and belonged to a traditional family, and the other who lives in the United States and works as a Reform cantor. I do not normally stumble on this disconnect until I go back home to Israel and visit with family and friends. While my closest friends fully accept what I do in the United States, some still operate within the restricted thought structure that comes from the primitive religious law in Israel. I myself do not always face the struggle between who I was and who I am today. I don't always have the patience to confront the criticisms and archaic reactions from Israelis who hear of what I do for a living. I still have work to do on unifying the two personalities, and to deal with the criticisms and strange looks. At times when I am in Israel, I feel myself regressing to that twenty-something-year-old person. Thank God I have my three girls to remind me that it isn't so. They are always there to provide a quick reality check, preventing me from reverting to the younger version of myself.

I hope to be able to bridge the gap between the different movements of Judaism as I have done within myself. There was a time in our not so distant past when all Jews were Jews without distinction. When Jews are persecuted, it doesn't matter what affiliations or belief systems we prefer. I'm a strong believer in the importance of *K'lal Yisrael*—the entire people of Israel as a single entity despite our different beliefs and practices. A Jewish adage says: *Kol Yisrael arevim ze la ze*—"All Israel is responsible for one another." I'd like to think that we can be less divided within our people, that we can care more for one another and spend less time judging each other's practices. I've learned that *K'lal Yisrael* is something that's difficult for people to attain. People easily speak but do not always act.

As an Israeli who grew up traditionally and was educated in the Reform movement in the United States, I want to help heal the divide caused by the ignorance of believing there is only one way to practice Judaism. Women, especially, can help lead the way to learn from one another. Judaism as a religion teaches community and togetherness. I believe we can have a stronger Judaism and Jewish identity by not only respecting and accepting our differences, but by learning from each other and celebrating our shared values and goals for the future.

Cantor Tamar Heather Havilio is the Head of Cantorial Studies and also serves as the Jerusalem Campus Senior Cantor at Hebrew Union College-Jewish Institute of Religion in Jerusalem, Israel. She is in her thirteenth year teaching and leading Prayer Workshops in the Year in Israel Program and the Israeli Rabbinic Program where she teaches future Rabbis, Cantors, and Jewish Educators of North America, Europe, and Israel.

She also holds an MA degree in Performance Studies from New York University and a Master's in Sacred Music and Cantorial Ordination from Hebrew Union College/Debbie Friedman School of Sacred Music in NYC. Tamar is building a new way of teaching prayer called "Trom-T'fillah" or Pre-Prayer in order to change the often mimetic way of past and current methods of teaching and learning prayer.

With this she is developing a new pedagogy of the prayer leader called, "The Praying Body." Tamar also is one of the prayer leaders of the Nashot haKotel (the Women of the Wall) and through prayer activism leads others in the voice of religious pluralism in Israel. She is married to Shmulik Havilio and they are the proud parents of three boys.

9
P*RESENT* T*AMAR*
Tamar Heather Havilio

I*N THE BEGINNING OF THE MOVIE* *Chocolat* a woman and her daughter come into a very traditional European town with the north wind. The town is basically stuck in time and repeats and repeats, again and again its own mantra of "tradition." The woman enters and opens a chocolate shop and literally spices her sweet chocolate delicacies with Mexican chilies. People stop in and enjoy, re-live stories and come to life. It is not only the decadent, spicy chocolates that entice and embody the townsfolk, but the woman's *joie-de-vivre* and charisma, which stop time and allow them to live life fuller and richer.

When I was a child about nine years old, I remember talking and praying to God in the tall evergreen trees in Eagle River, Wisconsin. I still find awe in those trees and search for that very essence of my childhood. Perhaps it was a sensation of the wind blowing, or the crushed leaves beneath my feet. It was that north wind that would bring a chill, even in late July. This presence was certainly bigger than me and greater than the trees. Whatever one calls it, I understood it to be a presence of God, and I started talking. It was this very memory of presence and of being in the moment that brought me to where I am today. The concept of presence is what forms my calling and my destination. I found it in my body as the present progressive now where I do not focus on what I will be doing next or what I just did, but rather on exactly what I am doing. Life became real in those moments and I followed the new paths that were revealed to me in the moment.

As in the movie *Chocolat*, that pure spirit that came out of the north wind and embodied the woman who brought the village to life, had embodied and consumed me. I was not only seeking the presence of God. I was on a passionate search in order to feel and live in the present progressive now, as it was later revealed to me: the Sabbath in the body.

I grew up in various places, but mostly in the state of Wisconsin. My parents divorced when I was very young and I only really remember them being separate. Both of my parents have shaped who I am and who I will be. It was the sense of love that filled my childhood days that kept me strong and curious. My mother, Mary, revealed to me the essence of presence when I was between the ages of nine and twelve. She was a pioneer in hospice. I do not remember specific stories of their lives, but I recall feeling the presence of people living out their last days. They were not sad or devastated as one could be, but rather so alive. I remember singing and laughing with them, and then one day knowing that they had died. The essence of life as temporal was also very real. As a young girl, I began my search for this sense of heightened awareness of living.

I tried to find this presence in the churches that I prayed in with my family. I remember praying so hard to God for all I could understand as holy and kind in the world. The singing inspired me and gave language to my personal prayer. The presence of God that dwelled in those awesome high trees in the Northwoods called me even stronger. The search for that specific heightened presence and awareness was made more urgent. In eighth grade I happened upon my other new religion, the theater. Mrs. Brown and the "Footlights' Flicks and Flashes" class brought me to a whole new level of living. I created films, wrote plays, and developed acting skills through life stories. I was putting life on the stage and in learning the worlds of theater, I found God as in those whistling trees up north. It was not just a period of coming of age, but also of coming to the presence of others in the "play." My friendships became deeper and more honest and my calling became clear. I was alive on the stage and my presence was wanted. The church's script became rote for me, but the theater scripts brought my soul to life in both a corporeal and spiritual way. I played many characters and learned many lines. Within the process of both rehearsal and performance I became a vessel for words that made me come to life. I went to theater and arts schools during the summers and grew to appreciate that my days would be filled with both on and off stage moments. The presence of the actor on stage was where I found the most real human connections. In the written text of any character on the page, I did not become a caricature of what I thought that person should be, but rather the many faces of me.

Although one can express many faces, one possesses only a single soul in a lifetime. My soul was definitely searching for holiness and God in both the tall trees in the north woods of Wisconsin, and in the theater where elevated presence was my lifeblood. I recall always finding that awesome essence in the trees and in the theater. Sometimes there was holiness, as Peter Brook wrote in his book, *The Empty Space: A Book About the Theatre: Deadly, Holy, Rough, Immediate.*[1] And other times, my fellow actors found *only* life and presence on the stage. They hid behind the role as a way to escape the simplicity of normalcy, or the deep complexity of their own souls. I remember struggling to find this holy theater that Brook longed for in his work. I realized also that the entire concept of presence was deeply connected to a shared longing for the idea of something holy—something purer and kinder than we now know. In theater, I was never satisfied with merely entertaining an audience. I wanted them to change, grow or struggle with me on the stage in a collective quest for the world to come, as a holier, more complete world.

Early on in theater school I learned more about teaching and learning presence through acting techniques and exercises of both Sanford Meisner and Jerzy Grotowski. In their techniques of training to find presence, I wanted to seek a theater for social change. In theater I found real life presence, but in real life I often just found the players in make believe time. The theater became my holy place where presence meant going out to the streets and revealing hypocrisies and inhumanity through the texts of Bertolt Brecht and the music of Kurt Weill.

I spent the second semester of my sophomore year in London studying this kind of theater. A little girl from Wisconsin was now encountering the politics of Margaret Thatcher's England and the working class struggle. In the neighborhood in North London where I lived, a Sephardic Jewish family befriended me. Their store was the only one open on Sundays, and they served traditional Middle Eastern food, which soon became my food. I added saffron, cumin, and cardamom spices to the shelf in my kitchen. The spices in my theater experience and in my cooking, like the Mexican chilies in the chocolate, enlightened my soul and awakened my Jewishness.

In the back of London's National Theatre in 1989, I saw the production of Joshua Sobol's play, *Ghetto*. I heard my Jewish soul on stage in the songs of the artist in the ghetto. The character's name was Chaya and she sang songs in order to stay alive. In the cabaret she sang of protest and love, which called upon my young spirit in a profound and life-changing way. I sat with her spirit and in time, as in a film, I knew a part of her was me and I was her. For a passing moment, I felt like I was on the stage singing her Yiddish songs as though they were mine. It was my life story as a struggling artist in politically uncertain times. I returned to Iowa that summer and found the local rabbi in order to continue seeking and finding this part of me that was now so alive. Judaism captured all that was me as a political theater artist and investigator of presence as an eternal quality within time.

While I studied in my conversion classes, I was also assistant director of the American premiere of a play about children in the ghetto. I was learning the religion and developing my Jewish knowledge through the journey of these children. I was given that task of teaching the children Hebrew prayers. I learned the prayer the night before and then taught them in rehearsal. These were my first b'nei mitzvah students and neither of us really knew. In this play, I also found my new name. The children in the play carried around a little rag doll named Tamar, which means "date," from the date palm that grows abundant in Israel. I also chose this name because of the story of Tamar and Yehudah. Not because it is the most innocent story. Tamar deceives Yehudah in order to have a child with him by disguising herself as a prostitute. Yet, by doing so, she chose her destiny. At that time, I also felt that my own destiny was in my hands.

I moved to Chicago next in order to pursue a career in the theater. There I studied the Meisner acting technique at the Actors Center. Sandford Meisner also believed in finding true presence in a scene and the text through repetition. It is first repetition of words that lead to subtext where two players create a scene. It was there that I also was reminded of the commercial aspects of "making it" in the theater world. I was aware of talent, but unaware of the cutthroat competition and, at times, downright unethical behavior in the name of theater. Obviously it was not the theater that I "prayed" in. I stayed in order to learn the technique and to find presence in a subtly Jewish way. Meisner, of course, grew up Jewish and I later found in my own work a striking similarity between the intention of repetition in Jewish prayer and his technique and quest for presence in acting. Later I found this as a way to teach presence in the prayer leader.

The Chicago area was a very powerful and influential place for me as a theater artist and eventually as a prayer leader. There is a tree on the Northwestern University Evanston campus that I planted with my "cherub" class of 1986 (NHSI High School program) that to this day I still visit. In that place I have struggled with life decisions and found presence in a young tree that reminded me to always stand tall with roots planted and reach out to the world with my branches. I suppose it was also the north wind that carried me to the North Shore of Chicago.

I lived on Cornelia Street in Lakeview, two blocks from Temple Sholom. I walked in one Shabbat evening and heard an angel singing. Cantor Aviva Katzman showed me a presence of a different and profound kind. In that moment I was drawn into a new holy theater. She took me under her wings and fed my hunger for more Jewish prayer and study. She led me to Hebrew Union College (HUC) in Jerusalem and then to the campus in Manhattan. It was at HUC where my quest for finding presence in the performance of prayer and the connection between the pedagogy of the theater practitioner and prayer leader became stronger than ever.

The first stop after Chicago was Israel in the summer of 1992. I remember stepping off the plane after hearing the mythical singing of *Heiveinu Shalom Aleichem* as I landed. It was summer and the air was hot. It was a different air than we have in Wisconsin. I was overwhelmed with both history and reality. I also recall that everyone around me was so incredibly beautiful and alive. There were women soldiers embracing a baby on one hip and a semi-automatic weapon on the other. There were tanned men with strong arms and smug smiles. It was certainly magical for me as a twenty-three year old. That year in Israel I discovered a deep longing of the relationship with God and the Jewish people in all kinds of Jerusalem stones.

The first Shabbat I had in Jerusalem, after a Kabbalat Shabbat service and dinner, a number of us walked to the Kotel later in the night. It must have been near 10:30 p.m. We entered through the Jewish quarter and I reached the top of the stairs before the plaza of the Western Wall and felt a tug towards the Kotel. I ran and ran and placed my hands upon those tall supernatural stones. Ubiquitous notes of tears and dirt crumbled beneath my fingers. I added wet tears of my own to this wall that I had never seen but had always known. I was truly home. This time with the warm wind from the east. The presence unseen through my hands and my praying body was quite unearthly, akin to a real-life out-of-body experience. I was not imagining this incredible feeling of *déjà-vu*. I had somehow, sometime, been there before. *Sh'ma Yisrael*. I prayed and went home with my new friends.

Upon returning to America, I had to imagine all of my memories of Israel from the balcony of my Upper West Side Manhattan apartment. I was still very much on a quest to understand the concept of learning and teaching presence. I was quickly learning, through my own relationship with the texts of Jewish prayer, that *l'hitpalel* (to pray) might be the original artist's gaze. The artist looks deep inside and struggles with herself before she turns the inside to the outside. She is self-reflexive, as in the reflexive verb form of *palel*.

At HUC the most prevailing question my classmates pondered was this: How does one lead prayer and pray at the same time? Again, I struggled with the fact that while we learned many texts, melodies and customs, we never really learned how to find and seek presence of one another and the "other" as God. In acting, the first exercise one learns is that each person must have a want or desire in the scene. I so wanted to find some sort of holiness in this increasingly chaotic world. The praying is first and the leading comes second. This desire in prayer is first and foremost in discovering presence. In those years of study, a seed began to develop in my gut to bring techniques of learning and teaching presence of the theater actor to the pray-*er* and prayer leader. I wanted to teach the desire to find presence by understanding one's own presence and then finding presence in the other.

My master's project at HUC delved into the world of the Golden Age of Cantors, when cantors performed simultaneously in the synagogue and the Yiddish Theater. I wanted to find the origins of the idea of the connection of presence in theater and prayer, and between the performance of the actor and of the prayer leader—when the prayer leader was the actor and *vice-versa*. As I dug further and deeper, my investigation went back to the biblical Purim play. Art and prayer has always been connected and now I understood how New York's Lower East Side of the 1920s became fertile ground for the development of this convergence of the two worlds. My favorite quote from my research is from Nahma Sandrow's book, *Vagabond Stars: The World History of the Yiddish Theater*: "And when the manager comes into the theater and sees the audience crying like Yom Kippur in synagogue, then he strokes his belly and goes home to sleep in peace, for he knows that this week he'll be able to pay wages and make a profit."[2] Here the commercial theater manager used the process of *doing* prayer as a way to draw his audience. This quote still inspires my work in training the prayer leader and in understanding the power of presence in prayer.

Upon being invested as a cantor in May of 1996, I took my first position in New Jersey. There I learned two things. First, how the performance of a prayer leader can also draw from the negative aspects of commercial theater when the actor becomes only for himself and personal gain. Second, how serious the need was for a new pedagogy of the prayer leader. My next position in my hometown of Milwaukee, Wisconsin saved my work and my cantorate. In November of 1999, I walked into a post-office to send a package and I saw the millennium clock before me. This was another life-changing moment. I discovered the holiness and reality of time "running." I saw the minutes and the seconds run on the clock and experienced a real panic. Perhaps it was also that I had turned thirty that year, and realized I needed to make some changes in my life in order to move on. The clock gave me a sense of the reality of time. It reminded me of the presence of the Sabbath and how perhaps Shabbat was really the body being in the present progressive now state in order to fully feel the experience or presence of others and the Wholly Other. In Milwaukee, I gained the courage to leave an unhappy marriage and pursue the work that perhaps I was made to do. In all of my research on the links between pedagogies of the theater practitioner and prayer leader, I found my own voice in the work of performance theorist and practitioner Richard Schechner of the Tisch School of the Arts, division of performance studies.

I remember learning about Richard Schechner's work at the University of Iowa. His picture is in the Alumni Hall of Fame. He developed the idea of performance studies in the drama department at New York University's Tisch School of the Arts. He combined theory and practice in his scholarly and artistic adventures. With his words, I suddenly felt answers to my own questions and the voice of a kindred spirit searching for the holiness of presence in all performance. I recall walking my dog Mazel late at night in a cold Milwaukee December and looking up to the stars in heaven and understanding that I had to study with Richard and connect the pedagogy of Jewish prayer and pedagogy of performing texts—ritual and otherwise.

I flew to New York and walked into Richard's office, following this northeast wind that drew me close. I began by explaining that I was an invested cantor from HUC, just two buildings over on Broadway and West Fourth Street, who began her journey as an experimental and political theater actor. I told him of my dream of somehow integrating the pedagogy of the presence of the performer into the pedagogy of presence in the prayer leader. I told him how sad I was that there was so much "bad" or over-produced theater in religious services. I also sang for him. I stood there and sang "Over the Rainbow." He told me about his entire Jewish background and his own struggle with Judaism and Israel. I told him that I believe that there must be a connection between Jewish prayer and the idea of theater as a transformative vehicle for change. I understood then that I had to study with Richard and was accepted into the program.

I had not yet moved back to New York City. It was May of 2000 and I was in Milwaukee. At a ceremony for Israel's Memorial Day, I met a man named Shmuel (Shmulik) Havilio. He had been invited by our community *sheliach* to speak about his brother-in-law Amir Zohar, who was the first reserve soldier killed in the Second Intifada. He spoke about Amir in memorial and I chanted the memorial prayer. Shmulik was so very gentle and handsome with deep sad brown eyes that were both calming and wise. He left a day later to return to Israel as I headed off to New York. I somehow knew that I would see those eyes again. Little did I know they would also be my children's eyes.

In August of 2001 I started the MA program at the Tisch School of the Art's division of performance studies. I was not on the path to combine the production and aesthetic aspects of theater and prayer, but rather the pedagogies of presence of the theater performer and the ritual Jewish performer. Then, on September 11th, all of our worlds changed. I will never forget that morning. It was a Tuesday, the day that I did not have classes at NYU. I came in from walking my dog and the doorman told me that two helicopters had crashed into the Twin Towers. I went up to my twelfth floor apartment and saw the first tower, and then the second tower just collapsed. It was so unreal, as if I was watching an awful movie or simulation of something gone awry. I did not have a television then, so I turned on the radio to listen to what the world was witnessing as a dreadful day in our history.

After the High Holy Days, my heart was again pulled to the east and, even though it was the height of the Second Intifada, I boarded a plane to Israel for Sukkot. I was called there in order to understand and be with a people who knew terror on a daily basis. I went to HUC in Jerusalem to say hello to all of my old teachers. I wanted to teach future prayer leaders and the idea of teaching at HUC entered my mind. I met with my teacher Cantor Dr. Eliyahu Schleifer, and he asked me if I would be interested in applying for a position. I felt as if someone were directing me to this work and to Israel. I understood again that presence in the Northwoods of Wisconsin when my body told me that I was encountering a presence that was holy and kind. I was following my gut instinct and discovered my calling. I returned to my studies at NYU and continued my investigation of pedagogy.

I met with Richard again, and he said to me, "I don't know if it's because suddenly there is a cantor on campus or because the Twin Towers just fell, but I want to discuss Jewish issues with you." With that we began to meet weekly and challenged each other on topics such as Israel and Jewish ritual. I was fascinated that Richard went all the way to India in order to research ritual performance and did not delve into his own Jewish roots. I asked him if I could take his work on performance and make it into a new pedagogy of Jewish prayer, and he agreed.

I explored the meaning of presence and the physical body in the present progressive and whether that could have been the original intention of Shabbat. In Richard's East Coast Artists Workshop, the idea of "Shabbat in the Body" came to me through his slow-motion exercise called "crossings." I am currently working on this as a way of teaching presence in Jewish prayer as the body slows down in silence and crosses a small place in an hour's time. This exercise is similar to "*shoheh*," or contemplatively waiting an hour before praying the *Amidah* (*Mishnah Brachot* 5:1). In the slowing down of the body, one experiences otherness in a profound way. This is the presence that I hoped to find again in order to help others to feel and understand the presence of one another and the Other as God.

Performance studies gave me the tools and the language in order to create a new way of teaching presence in the body. In the spring of 2002, HUC in Jerusalem asked me if I would be interested in coming to teach and work with Professor Schleifer in the cantorial studies program. This was a very tense time in Israel—the height of the Second Intifada—but I somehow knew it was right. I emailed my friend, Shmulik Havilio, and told him that I would be moving to Israel at the conclusion of my studies at NYU in August of 2002. We had been in email contact earlier in the year when I asked him about Shabbat in Jerusalem. He told me that he always appreciated the "stop time" in the air on Friday when Shabbat begins. I prepared myself all summer for my big real-life adventure. I wanted to teach future prayer leaders and Jerusalem called me. It seemed as if a door was opening with the very north wind felt in the movie *Chocolat*—except this wind was calling me from the east.

I boarded an EL AL flight to Tel Aviv from Newark with my eighty-five pound golden retriever, Mazel, and Shmulik Havilio picked us up at Ben Gurion Airport. He was and still is my Prince Charming in the body of a twentieth-generation (800 years) Jerusalemite. His family originally came from the Basque country in Northern Spain. The family forefather, Yekhiel Avraham Ben-Haim Havilio, was expelled from Spain in the thirteenth century for having theological discussions with Christians and migrated to Eretz Yisrael. He was buried on the Mount of Olives in 1265. On our second date in Jerusalem, Shmulik took me to the Havilio Square in downtown Jerusalem, where for 300 years they had a candy factory. Like Tamar in the story of Tamar and Yehudah, I knew at that moment that I had to choose my destiny with this man of great history and honor.

In my story, we chose each other: a twentieth-generation Jerusalemite and an American descendant of the second Mayflower. We were married in the garden at HUC on July 18, 2004 following our Orthodox or "state" wedding in the Sephardic synagogue of Yemin Moshe, Jerusalem on July 4th.

I am beginning my twelfth year teaching at HUC. Shmulik and I have three gorgeous boys: Nadav, Tal and Noam. Each day that I teach in the prayer workshop, I strive to give students tools in order to both desire presence of the other and the Other as God. I call God the "big unknown" that we have to give space to in order to dwell within and among us as presence. I teach that prayer leaders must have a "want" in prayer and the ability to "eat" the text and give the text back to the congregation in a very authentic and honest way.

In my praying body workshop, I place students in slow-motion movement exercises so that they have the capacity to hear their internal time clocks and prayers, as in the silent prayer of Hannah in First Samuel. This is prayer that is initiated within the belly. I am also utilizing the work of my professor Richard Schechner's Indian rasa boxes (rasaboxes.com) in order to develop a physical way to teach textual embodiment through the specific emotional connection to a prayer text. I pray that I can emulate for my students what I teach as my own authentic prayer. My personal mantra is posted at the entrance to the Schatz House in Jerusalem where the famous sculptor Boris Schatz lived. It says: "Art without soul is like prayer without intention." I am trying to teach this entrance to the soul and subtext of one's very personal prayer that brings to life the words on the page of the prayer book.

I also teach with my feet, or as Rabbi Abraham Joshua Heschel would say, "pray with my feet." Earlier this year when Anat Hoffman, the leader of the organization the Women of the Wall, was arrested for praying with a *talit* (prayer shawl) at the Western Wall, I decided that I wanted to help the cause. I asked Anat what exactly I could do, and she said that I could be the prayer leader for Rosh Chodesh Kislev. I felt extremely honored and blessed. Perhaps some singers dream of Carnegie Hall, but

I dreamed of singing and praying in full voice at the Kotel. The presence in that place is for me quite like the presence in the Northwoods of Wisconsin.

I woke up at 5:00 a.m. in order to arrive at the Kotel by 6:45. I went straight up to the stones and placed my hands upon them. It was the feeling of tears on my face again and an overwhelming sense that the thousands of years of women's tears were falling with me. I stood in the middle of the members of Women of the Wall and opened my mouth and the prayers flowed out strong. My voice bounced off of the wall and seemed even more amplified. It was like a dream and I thought that someone would wake me up. I never in my lifetime thought that I would pray as a *chazzan* at the Kotel. Last month I stood next to my dear students and one of them, Jennifer, even sang a duet with me at the Wall. I felt something indeed bigger than all of us. The essence of the life-giving woman from the film *Chocolat* was somehow breathed into me and I am so grateful.

I have learned and pray that I teach how to give presence and dwell in the presence of others. Presence and the present progressive now are deeply embedded in my DNA. The Sabbath as a strike of the body, which constantly wants to dwell in the future or past, sits in the present progressive now *in* the Sabbath. Here in Israel I feel the presence of the Sabbath as she enters my home on Friday evening. The wind blows in the feeling of stop-time and I light the candles, cover my eyes, sing the blessing and taste the time. I am home.

Notes

1. Peter Brook, *The Empty Space: A Book About the Theatre: Deadly, Holy, Rough, Immediate* (New York: Touchstone, 1995).

2. Nahma Sandrow, *Vagabond Stars: A World History of Yiddish Theater* (Syracuse: Syracuse University Press, 1996), 261.

About the Editors

Jonathan L. Friedmann

is a cantor, composer, biblical scholar, and musicologist. He received Cantorial Ordination and a Masters in Jewish Sacred Music from the Academy for Jewish Religion, California, where he is currently Professor of Jewish Music History. He also holds B.A. and M.A. degrees in Religious Studies from California State University, Long Beach, and a Ph.D. in Hebrew Bible from the joint program of North-West University and Greenwich School of Theology.

He has published hundreds of popular and peer-reviewed articles on music and religion and has authored or edited over a dozen books, including *Synagogue Song: An Introduction to Concepts, Theories, and Customs* (McFarland), *Social Functions of Synagogue Song: A Durkheimian Approach* (Lexington) and *Music in the Hebrew Bible: Understanding References in the Torah, Nevi'im and Ketuvim* (McFarland).

In addition to teaching at the Academy for Jewish Religion, California, Jonathan also is:

• Cantor of Bet Knesset Bamidbar, Las Vegas, NV

• Community Leader & Education Director of Adat Chaverim Cong. for Humanistic Judaism in Los Angeles

• Historical Music Editor for the *Western States Jewish History Journal*.

Meeka Simerly

was born in Haifa, Israel, and was raised in an ultra-secular Zionist environment. After moving to the United States in 1995 she discovered her Jewish religious roots, becoming musically active in congregations and Jewish organizations in Silicon Valley. She earned her B.A. *cum laude* in music education from San Jose State University in 2004, and received her Cantorial Ordination and a Masters in Jewish Sacred Music from the Academy for Jewish Religion, California in 2009. She was recently accepted to the rabbinic program at her alma mater, where she will continue her studies toward becoming a rabbi.

Cantor Simerly has been serving as the Cantor of Temple Emanu-El of San Jose since 2006. In addition to providing spiritual worship experiences for TEE's congregants, Cantor Simerly officiates at life cycle events, and shares the love of Torah and sacred text-study with children and adults of all ages. Her essay, "Naomi Shemer's Artistic Expression: Poetry, Prayer, or Both?" was published in *Emotions in Jewish Music: Personal and Scholarly Reflections* (University Press of America, 2012).

For more about Cantor Simerly see page 78.

SELECTED BIBLIOGRAPHY

The academic study of women in Judaism began in the mid-1970s. It has since blossomed into a multidisciplinary scholarly and applied field. Included in this bibliography are works representing the most widely covered areas: biblical commentary and criticism; rabbinic literature and law; spirituality and mysticism; history and sociology (United States and Israel); feminism and gender studies; personal stories and reflections; and ritual studies.

Adelman, Penina. *Miriam's Well: Rituals for Jewish Women Around the Year.* Mount Vernon, NY: Biblio, 1996.

————. ed. *Praise Her Works: Conversations with Biblical Women.* Philadelphia: Jewish Publication Society, 1995.

Adler, Rachel. *Engendering Judaism: An Inclusive Theology and Ethics.* Boston: Beacon Press, 1999.

Alexander, Elizabeth Shanks. *Gender and Timebound Commandments in Judaism.* New York: Cambridge University Press, 2013.

Anisfeld, Sharon Cohen, Tara Mohr, and Catherine Spector, ed. *The Women's Passover Companion: Women's Reflections on the Festival of Freedom.* Woodstock, VT: Jewish Lights, 2003.

Antler, Joyce. *The Journey Home: Jewish Women and the American Century.* New York: Simon and Schuster, 1997.

Baker, Adrienne. *The Jewish Woman in Contemporary Society: Transitions and Traditions.* New York: Palgrave Macmillan, 1993.

Baskin, Judith Reesa. *Jewish Women in Historical Perspective.* Detroit: Wayne State University Press, 1998.

————. *Midrashic Women: Formations of the Feminine in Rabbinic Literature.* Hanover, MA: Brandeis University Press, 2002.

Baskin, Judith Reesa, and Shelly Tenenbaum, ed. *Gender and Jewish Studies: A Curriculum Guide.* Mount Vernon, NY: Biblio, 1994.

Berkovic, Sally. *Straight Talk: My Dilemma as an Orthodox Jewish Woman.* New York: KTAV, 1997.

Berkovits, Eliezer. *Jewish Women in Time and Torah.* New York: KTAV, 1990.

Berwin, Mel, and Jennifer Sartori. *Making Our Wilderness Bloom: Women Who Made American Jewish History.* Brookline, MA: Jewish Women's Archive, 2004.

Biale, Rachel. *Women and Jewish Law: The Essential Texts, Their History, and Their Relevance for Today*. New York: Random House, 2008.

Brayer, Menachem M. *The Jewish Woman in Rabbinic Literature: A Psychological Perspective*. New York: KTAV, 1986.

Brenner, Athalya, and Carole R. Fontaine, ed. *A Feminist Companion to Reading the Bible: Approaches, Methods and Strategies*. New York: Taylor and Francis, 2011.

Bronner, Leila Leah. *From Eve to Esther: Rabbinic Reconstructions of Biblical Women*. Louisville, KY: Westminster John Knox, 1994.

Brown, Cheryl Anne. *No Longer Be Silent: First Century Jewish Portraits of Biblical Women*. Louisville, KY: Westminster John Knox, 1992.

Burstein, Janet. *Writing Mothers, Writing Daughters: Tracing the Maternal in Stories by American Jewish Women*. Champaign: University of Illinois Press, 1996.

Buxbaum, Yitzhak. *Jewish Tales of Holy Women*. San Francisco: Jossey-Bass, 2002.

Cantor, Aviva. *Jewish Women/Jewish Men: The Legacy of Patriarchy in Jewish Life*. San Francisco: HarperSanFrancisco, 1995.

Carney, Janet, Ruth Ann Magder, Laura Wine Paster, and Marcia Cohn Spiegel. *The Jewish Women's Awareness Guide: Connections for the 2nd Wave of Jewish Feminism*. New York: Bloch, 1997.

Chesler, Phyllis, and Rivka Haut, ed. *Women of the Wall: Claiming Sacred Ground at Judaism's Holy Site*. Woodstock, VT: Jewish Lights, 2003.

Cohen, Shaye J. D. *Why Aren't Jewish Women Circumcised? Gender and Covenant in Judaism*. Berkeley: University of California Press, 2005.

Dame, Enid, Lilly Rivlin, and Henry Wenkart. *Which Lilith? Feminist Writers Re-create the World's First Woman*. Northvale, NJ: Jason Aronson, 1998.

Davidman, Lynn. *Tradition in a Rootless World: Women Turn to Orthodox Judaism*. Berkeley: University of California Press, 1991.

Davidman, Lynn, and Shelly Tenenbaum, ed. *Feminist Perspectives on Jewish Studies*. New Haven, CT: Yale University Press, 1994.

Desen, Shlomo, Charles Seymour Liebman and Moshe Shokeid, ed. *Israeli Judaism: The Sociology of Religion in Israel*. New Brunswick, NJ: Transaction, 1995.

Devine, Luke. *From Anglo-First-Wave Towards American Second-Wave Jewish Feminism: Negotiating With Jewish Feminist Theology and Its Communities in the Writing of Amy Levy*. Piscataway, NJ: Gorgias, 2010.

Diner, Hasia, Shira Kohn and Rachel Kranson. *A Jewish Feminine Mystique? Jewish Women in Postwar America*. New Brunswick, NJ: Rutgers University Press, 2010.

Drucker, Malka, ed. *Women and Judaism*. Westport, CT: Praeger, 2009.

Dzmura, Noach. *Balancing on the Mechitza: Transgender in Jewish Community*. Berkeley, CA: North Atlantic, 2010.

Elior, Rachel. *Men and Women: Gender, Judaism and Democracy*. Jerusalem: Urim, 2005.

Elper, Ora Wiskind and Susan A. Handelman, ed. *Torah of the Mothers: Contemporary Jewish Women Read Classical Jewish Texts*. Jerusalem: Urim, 2000.

Eskenazi, Tamara Cohn, and Andrea L. Weiss. *The Torah: A Women's Commentary*. New York: Union for Reform Judaism, 2007.

Fader, Ayala. *Mitzvah Girls: Bringing Up the Next Generation of Hasidic Jews in Brooklyn*. Princeton, NJ: Princeton University Press, 2009.

Feld, Merle. *Spiritual Life: A Jewish Feminist Journey*. New York: SUNY Press, 1999.

Felder, Deborah G., and Diana Rosen. *Fifty Jewish Women Who Changed the World*. New York: Citadel, 2003.

Firestone, Tirzah. *The Receiving: Reclaiming Jewish Women's Wisdom*. New York: HarperCollins, 2009.

Fishman, Sylvia Barack. *A Breath of Life: Feminism in the American Jewish Community*. Hanover, MA: Brandeis University Press, 1995.

Frankel, Ellen. *Five Books of Miriam: A Woman's Commentary on the Torah*. New York: HarperCollins, 1997.

Frankel, Jonathan. *Jews and Gender: The Challenge to Hierarchy*. New York: Oxford University Press, 2001.

Frankiel, Tamar. *The Voice of Sarah: Feminine Spirituality and Traditional Judaism*. San Francisco: HarperSan Francisco, 1990.

Fuchs, Esther, ed. *Israeli Feminist Scholarship: Gender, Zionism, and Difference*. Austin: University of Texas Press, 2014.

Fuchs, Ilan. *Jewish Women's Torah Study: Orthodox Religious Education and Modernity*. New York: Routledge, 2013.

Ghatan, H. E. Yedidiah. *The Invaluable Pearl: The Unique Status of Women in Judaism*. New York: Bloch, 1986.

Goldstein, Elyse. *Revisions: Seeing Torah Through a Feminist Lens*. Woodstock, VT: Jewish Lights, 2001.

_____. *Seek Her Out: A Textual Approach to the Study of Women and Judaism*. New York: Union for Reform Judaism, 2003.

_____, ed. *The Women's Haftarah Commentary: New Insight from Women Rabbis on the 54 Haftarah Portions, the 5 Megillot & Special Shabbatot*. Woodstock, VT: Jewish Lights, 2008.

_____, ed. *The Women's Torah Commentary: New Insights from Women Rabbis on the 54 Weekly Torah Portions*. Woodstock, VT: Jewish Lights, 2008.

Goldstein, Elyse, and Anita Diamant, ed. *New Jewish Feminism: Probing the Past, Forging the Future*. Woodstock, VT: Jewish Lights, 2008.

Gottlieb, Lynn. *She Who Dwells Within: Feminist Vision of a Renewed Judaism*. New York: HarperCollins, 1995.

Graetz, Naomi. *Unlocking the Garden: A Feminist Jewish Look at the Bible, Midrash and God*. Piscataway, NJ: Gorgias, 2005.

Greenberg, Blu. *On Women & Judaism: A View from Tradition*. Philadelphia: Jewish Publication Society, 1981.

Greenspahn, Frederick E, ed. *Women and Judaism: New Insights and Scholarship*. New York: NYU Press, 2009.

Grossman, Susan, and Rivka Haut, ed. *Daughters of the King: Women and the Synagogue*. Philadelphia: Jewish Publication Society, 2005.

Haberman, Bonna Devora. *Israeli Feminism Liberating Judaism: Blood and Ink*. Lanham, MD: Lexington, 2012.

Haddad, Yvonne Yazbeck, and John L. Esposito, ed. *Daughters of Abraham: Feminist Thought in Judaism, Christianity, and Islam*. Gainsville: University Press of Florida, 2001.

Halpern, Michael D., and Chana Safrai, ed. *Jewish Legal Writings by Women*. Jerusalem: Urim, 1998.

Hartman, Tova. *Feminism Encounters Traditional Judaism: Resistance and Accommodation*. Hanover, MA: Brandeis University Press, 2007.

Hauptman, Judith. *Rereading The Rabbis: A Woman's Voice*. Boulder, CO: Westview, 2008.

Heller, Tziporah. *Our Bodies, Our Souls: A Jewish Perspective on Feminine Spirituality*. Jerusalem: Targum, 2003.

Henkin, J. H. *Responsa on Contemporary Jewish Women's Issues*. New York: KTAV, 2003.

Heschel, Susannah. *On Being a Jewish Feminist*. New York: Schocken, 1995.

Hoshen, Dalia. *Beruria the Tannait: A Theological Reading of a Female Mishnaic Scholar*. Lanham, MD: University Press of America, 2007.

Irshai, Ronit. *Fertility and Jewish Law: Feminist Perspectives on Orthodox Responsa Literature*. Hanover, MA: Brandeis University Press, 2012.

Israel-Cohen, Yael. *Between Feminism and Orthodox Judaism: Resistance, Identity, and Religious Change in Israel*. Boston: Brill, 2012.

Kabakov, Miryam, ed. *Keep Your Wives Away from Them: Orthodox Women, Unorthodox Desires: An Anthology*. Berkeley, CA: North Atlantic, 2010.

Kaplan, Marion A., and Deborah Dash Moore, ed. *Gender and Jewish History*. Bloomington: Indiana University Press, 2011.

Kark, Ruth, Margalit Shilo, Galit Hasan-Rokem, and Shulamit Reinharz. *Jewish Women in Pre-State Israel: Life History, Politics, and Culture*. Hanover, MA: Brandeis University Press, 2008.

Kates, Judith A. *Reading Ruth: Contemporary Women Reclaim a Sacred Story*. New York: Ballantine, 1994.

Kaufman, Debra R. *Rachel's Daughters: Newly Orthodox Jewish Women*. New Brunswick, NJ: Rutgers University Press, 1991.

Kay, Evelyn. *The Hole in the Sheet: A Modern Woman Looks at Orthodox and Hasidic Judaism*. Secaucus, NJ: L. Stuart, 1987.

Keller, Rosemary Skinner, and Rosemary Radford Ruether, ed. *In Our Own Voices: Four Centuries of American Women's Religious Writing*. Louisville, KY: Westminster John Knox, 1995.

Klepfisz, Irena. *Dreams of an Insomniac: Jewish Feminist Essays, Speeches and Diatribes*. Portland, OR: Eighth Mountain, 1993.

Koltun, Elizabeth. *The Jewish Woman: New Perspectives*. New York: Schocken, 1976.

Kornbluth, Doron, ed. *Jewish Women Speak about Jewish Matters*. Jerusalem: Targum, 2008.

Krakower, Dora Brenner. *Trusting the Song that Sings Within: Pioneer Woman Cantor*. Ontario: Azure, 1997.

Landau, Melanie. *Tradition and Equality in Jewish Marriage: Beyond the Sanctification of Subordination*. New York: Bloomsbury Academic, 2012.

Landress, Barbara. *Her Glory All Within: Rejecting and Transforming Orthodoxy in Israeli and American Jewish Women's Fiction*. Boston: Academic Studies, 2012.

Lavie, Aliza, ed. *A Jewish Woman's Prayer Book*. New York: Random House, 2008.

Lederhendler, Eli, ed. *Who Owns Judaism? Public Religion and Private Faith in America and Israel*. New York: Oxford University Press, 2001.

Levitt, Laura. *Jews and Feminism: The Ambivalent Search for Home*. Philadelphia: Psychology, 1997.

Linett, Maren Tova. *Modernism, Feminism, and Jewishness*. New York: Cambridge University Press, 2010.

Meiselman, Moshe. *Jewish Woman in Jewish Law*. New York: KTAV, 1978.

Millen, Rochelle L. *Women, Birth, and Death in Jewish Law and Practice*. Hanover, MA: Brandeis University Press, 2004.

Misra, Kalpana, and Melanie Rich, ed. *Jewish Feminism in Israel: Some Contemporary Perspectives*. Hanover, MA: Brandeis University Press, 2003.

Moore, Tracy, ed. *Lesbiot: Israeli Lesbians Talk About Sexuality, Feminism, Judaism and Their Lives*. London: Cassell, 1999.

Morris, Bonnie J. *Lubavitcher Women in America: Identity and Activism in the   Postwar Era*. New York: SUNY Press, 1998.

Nadell, Pamela S. *Women Who Would Be Rabbis: A History of Women's Ordination 1889-1985*. Boston: Beacon, 1999.

Nadell, Pamela S., and Jonathan D. Sarna, ed. *Women and American Judaism: Historical Perspectives*. Hanover, MA: Brandeis University Press, 2001.

Nissel, Menachem. *Rigshei Lev: Women and Tefillah: Perspectives, Laws, and Customs*. Jerusalem: Targum, 2001.

Novick, Leah. *On the Wings of Shekhinah: Rediscovering Judaism's Divine Feminine*. Wheaton, IL: Quest, 2008.

Ochs, Vanessa L. *Sarah Laughed: Modern Lessons from the Wisdom and Stories of Biblical Women*. Philadelphia: Jewish Publication Society, 2011.

Orenstein, Debora, and Jane Rachel Litman, ed. *Lifecycles: Jewish Women on Life Passages and Personal Milestones*. Woodstock, VT: Jewish Lights, 1998.

Orenstein, Walter. *The Cantor's Manual of Jewish Law*. Northvale, NJ: Jason Aronson, 1994.

Paloma, Vanessa. *Mystic Siren: Woman's Voice in the Balance of Creation*. Santa Fe, NM: Gaon Books, 2007.

Partnow, Elaine Bernstein, ed. *The Quotable Jewish Woman: Wisdom, Inspiration & Humor from the Mind and Heart*. Woodstock, VT: Jewish Lights, 2007.

Peskowitz, Miriam, and Laura Levitt. *Judaism Since Gender*. New York: Routledge, 1997.

Pinsky, Dina. *Jewish Feminists: Complex Identities and Activist Lives*. Champaign: University of Illinois Press, 2009.

Plaskow, Judith. *Standing Again at Sinai: Judaism from a Feminist Perspective*. New York: HarperCollins, 1991.

Plaskow, Judith, and Donna Berman, ed. *The Coming of Lilith: Essays on Feminism, Judaism, and Sexual Ethics, 1972-2003*. Boston: Beacon, 2005.

Pogrebin, Letty. *Deborah, Golda, and Me*. New York: Anchor, 2011.

Prell, Riv-Ellen, ed. *Women Remaking American Judaism*. Detroit: Wayne State University Press, 2007.

Priesand, Sally. *Judaism and the New Woman*. New York: Behrman House, 1975.

Rogow, Faith. *Gone to Another Meeting: The National Council of Jewish Women, 1893-1993*. Tuscaloosa: University of Alabama Press, 1993.

Rom, Michal, and Orly Benjamin. *Feminism, Family, and Identity in Israel: Women's Marital Names*. New York: Palgrave Macmillan, 2011.

Rosen, Norma. *Biblical Women Unbound: Counter-Tales*. Philadelphia: Jewish Publication Society, 2010.

Ross, Tamar. *Expanding the Palace of Torah: Orthodoxy and Feminism*. Hanover: Brandeis University Press, 2004.

Rothschild, Sylvia, and Sybil Sheridan. *Taking Up the Timbrel: The Challenge of Creating Ritual for Jewish Women Today*. London: SCM, 2000.

Rudavsky, Tamar, ed. *Gender and Judaism: The Transformation of Tradition*. New York: NYU Press, 1995.

Ruether, Rosemary Radford, and Eleanor McLaughlin. *Women of Spirit: Female Leadership in the Jewish and Christian Traditions*. Eugene, OR: Wipf & Stock,1998.

Ruttenberg, Danya. *Surprised by God: How I Learned to Stop Worrying and Love Religion*. Boston: Beacon, 2009.

_____, ed. *Yentl's Revenge: The Next Wave of Jewish Feminism*. Seattle, WA: Seal, 2001.

Sacks, Maurie, ed. *Active Voices: Women in Jewish Culture*. Champaign: University of Illinois Press, 1995.

Sassoon, Isaac. *The Status of Women in Jewish Tradition*. New York: Cambridge University Press, 2011.

Schneider, Susan Weidman. *Jewish and Female: Choices and Changes in Our Lives Today*. New York: Simon and Schuster, 1984.

Schwartz, Shuly. *The Rabbi's Wife: The Rebbetzin in American Jewish Life*. New York: NYU Press, 2007.

Shepherd, Naomi. *A Price Below Rubies: Jewish Women as Rebels and Radicals*. Cambridge: Harvard University Press, 1993.

Siegel, Rachel J., Ellen Cole, and Esther D Rothblum. *Celebrating the Lives of Jewish Women: Patterns in a Feminist Sampler*. New York: Routledge, 1997.

Slonim, Rivkah, and Liz Rosenberg. *Bread and Fire: Jewish Women Find God in the Everyday*. Jerusalem: Urim, 2008.

Sokoloff, Naomi B., Anne Lapidus Lerner, and Anita Norich, ed. *Gender and Text in Modern Hebrew and Yiddish Literature*. New York: Jewish Theological Seminary, 1994.

Sperber, Daniel, Mendel Shapiro, Eliav Shochetman, and Shlomo Riskin. *Women and Men in Communal Prayer: Halakhic Perspectives*. New York: KTAV, 2010.

Swartz, Sarah Silberstein, and Margie Wolfe, ed. *From Memory to Transformation: Jewish Women's Voices.* Toronto: Second Story, 1998.

Swidler, Leonard J. *Biblical Affirmations of Woman.* Louisville, KY: Westminster John Knox, 1979.

————. *Women in Judaism: The Status of Women in Formative Judaism.* Metuchen, NJ: Scarecrow Press, 1976.

Tirosh-Samuelson, Hava, ed. *Women and Gender in Jewish Philosophy.* Bloomington: Indiana University Press, 2004.

Tuchman, Shera Aranoff, and Sandra E. Rapoport. *Moses' Women.* New York: KTAV, 2008.

Umansky, Ellen M., and Dianne Ashton, ed. *Four Centuries of Jewish Women's Spirituality: A Sourcebook.* Hanover, MA: Brandeis University Press, 2009.

Vincent, Isabel. *Bodies and Souls: The Tragic Plight of Three Jewish Women Forced into Prostitution in the Americas.* New York: HarperCollins, 2006.

Wegner, Judith Romney. *Chattel Or Person? The Status of Women in the Mishnah.* New York: Oxford University Press, 1992.

Weiss, Avraham. *Women at Prayer: A Halakhic Analysis of Women's Prayer Groups.* New York: KTAV, 2001.

Weissler, Chava. *Voices of the Matriarchs: Listening to the Prayers of Early Modern Jewish Women.* Boston: Beacon Press, 1999.

Wolowelsky, Joel B., ed. *Women, Jewish Law and Modernity: New Opportunities in a Post-feminist Age.* New York: KTAV, 1997.

————, ed. *Women and the Study of Torah: Essays from the Pages of Tradition.* New York: KTAV, 2001.

Zimmerman, Akiva. *S'harei Ron: The Cantorate in Responsa.* Tel Aviv: Bron Yahad, 1992.

Zlotnick, Helena. *Dinah's Daughters: Gender and Judaism from the Hebrew Bible to Late Antiquity.* Philadelphia: University of Pennsylvania Press, 2002.

Zola, Gary Phillip, ed. *Women Rabbis: Exploration & Celebration: Papers Delivered at an Academic Conference Honoring Twenty Years of Women in the Rabbinate, 1972-1992.* New York: Hebrew Union College Press, 1996.

GAON BOOKS
Jewish Women's Voices

- Gloria Abella Ballen. 2014. *The Power of the Hebrew Alphabet.* **Winner Best Book in Religion 2014** (New Mexico/Arizona Book Awards); **2014 National Jewish Book Award Nominee,** Jewish Book Council.
  - Angelina Muñiz-Huberman. 2014. *Dreaming of Safed.*
  - _____. 2010. *The Confidantes.*
  - Patricia Gottlieb Shapiro. 2013. *The Privilege of Aging: Portraits of Twelve Jewish Women.* **Finalist Best Book Award. 2014. Jewish Book Council Selection for the Author's Network 2013.**
  - Susana Weich-Shahak. 2013. *Moroccan Sephardic Romancero: Anthology of an Oral Tradition.* **Winner of European Folklore Prize and Finalist Best Book Award 2014.**
  - Ruth Sohn. 2013. *Crossing Cairo: A Jewish Woman's Encounter with Egypt.* **Finalist Best Book Award 2013. Jewish Book Council Selection for the Author's Network 2013.**
  - Vanessa Paloma. 2011. *The Mountain, the Desert and the Pomegranate: Stories from Morocco and Beyond.* **Finalist Best Book Award, 2012.**
  - _____. 2007. Mystic Siren: Woman's Voice in the Balance of Creation.
  - Anne. F. Schlezinger. 2011. *Pulling It All Together: Diary by One of America's First Jewish Women Federal Judges.*
  - Rabbi Min Kantrowitz. 2011. *Counting the Omer: A Kabbalistic Meditation Guide.* Selected as **"Book of Note" by the Jewish Book World.**
  - Susan Vorhand. 2009. *The Mosaic Within: An Alchemy of Healing Self and Soul.* **Finalist Best Book Award. Winner Best Book Design.**

Gaon Books
in association with
Gaon Institute for Tolerance Studies
a 501-c-3 organization
Education about Jewish Life, Thought & Diversity
www.gaoninstitute.org

CPSIA information can be obtained
at www.ICGtesting.com
Printed in the USA
LVHW11s0343181018
593997LV00002B/336/P